St. Botolph without Aldersgate

Parish of St. Botolph Without Aldersgate

A Statement of all Charities Connected With the Parish ...

St. Botolph without Aldersgate

Parish of St. Botolph Without Aldersgate
A Statement of all Charities Connected With the Parish ...

ISBN/EAN: 9783744788632

Printed in Europe, USA, Canada, Australia, Japan

Cover: Foto ©ninafisch / pixelio.de

More available books at **www.hansebooks.com**

PARISH

OF

ST. BOTOLPH WITHOUT ALDERSGATE.

A STATEMENT

OF

ALL CHARITIES

CONNECTED WITH THE PARISH,

AND

THEIR ANNUAL VALUE

WHEN BEQUEATHED, AND ON THE 25th MARCH, 1865.

ALSO

A RETURN OF PARISH ESTATES,

(WITH THE NAMES AND ADDRESSES OF TRUSTEES,)

HOW ACQUIRED, AND THEIR ANNUAL VALUES

AT THE DATE OF ACQUISITION, AND AT MARCH 1865,

AND

HOW EACH HAVE BEEN APPROPRIATED,

(As far as by-gone time will allow.)

WILLIAM WALLFORD, } *Churchwardens.*
HENRY DIGBY,

J. R. CUTTS, *Vestry Clerk.*

11, Charterhouse Square, E.C.

J. C. LARRANCE, PRINTER,
94, Aldersgate Street.

INDEX
1373713

	PAGE
Acton's, James, Charity	84
Adams's Richard and Margaret, Charity	25
128, Aldersgate-street	132, 178
129, "	132, 178
140, "	138, 168, 178
141, "	138, 168, 178
142, "	139, 168, 178
164, "	133, 150, 178
165, "	134, 150, 155, 178
166, "	135, 155, 178
167, "	135, 155, 178
Allington's, George, Charity	107
Altham's, Sir James, Charity	107
Anderson's, Sir Henry, Charity	75
Black Horse Alley	138-9, 165-8
Bowman's Buildings	168, 178
Bude's, Richard, Charity	95
Carter's, John, Charity	119
Church House	132, 142, 147, 178
Cloth Fair	142, 147, 178
Conyers's, John, Charity	26
Court's, William, Charity	105
Crippes's, Robert, Charity	24
Crooked Billet	133, 178
Cureton's, H. O., Charity	126
Dane's, Margaret, Charity	29
Dawtrey's Charity	28
Doolittle Lane Premises	140, 172, 178
Edward the Sixth's, King, Charity	111
Estates, Summary of	178
Fyer's, Henry, Charity	63
Gadbury's, Richard, Charity	18
Glassbrooke's, James, Charity	80
Godwin's, Nicholas, Charity	93
Hibben's, Elizabeth, Charity	113
Holeman's, Philip, Charity	102
Hyde's, Barnard, Charity	115
Jenkins's, Jane, Charity	103
Johnson's, Alleyne, premises	150
Kempster's, Matthew, Charity	175
King Edward the Sixth's Charity	111

	PAGE
Leake's, Henry, Charity	109
Little Britain, 77	137, 178
" 77½	137, 161, 178
" 81	178
Little Knight Rider Court 5 & 6, 140, 172-8
Loggin's, Robert, Charity	87
Maidenhead Alley	162-3, 178
" Court, 4, 5, 6, 7, and 8	137, 178
Metcalfe's, Thomas, Charity	106
Minister's House	137, 161, 178
Morley's, John, Charity	17
Mynn's, John, Charity	90
Necton's House	168
New College, Oxford	144-7
Normansed's, Richard, Charity	20
Osmotherlaw's, Richard, Charity	176
Packington's, Dame Ann, Charity	5
" " by Deed	121
Pease's, William, Charity	23
Petty Wales Estate	144, 178
Property, List of Parish	178
Purden's, Katherine, Charity	96
Ramsey's, Lady, Charity	114
Roberts's, Tedder, Charity	99
Skydmore's, Stephen, Charity	11
Smith's, Alderman, Charity	32
Snow's, Thomas, Charity	21
Summary of Parish Property	178
Swayne's, William, Charity	108
Tamworth's, Christopher, Charity	12, 142-8
Taylor's, Roger, Charity	19
Thornbury's, William, Charity	91
Trinity Hall	55, 135, 136, 155, 178
Trust Deed, 17th November, 1865	128
Trustees Under Deed, 17th November, 1865	3
Turner's, Thomas, Charity	120
Ward's, Mrs., Charity	22
Westwood's, Humfrie, Charity	100
Wotton's, John, Charity	107

PARISH

OF

ST. BOTOLPH WITHOUT ALDERSGATE.

At a General Vestry of the Parish,
HOLDEN AT SHAFTESBURY HALL, 36, ALDERSGATE STREET,
On the 14th day of June, 1866,

The REVEREND W. C. F. WEBBER, in the Chair,

IT WAS MOVED by Mr. J. W. Lowick,
Seconded by Mr. W. Wallford, and

RESOLVED

"That the 'Vestry Clerk' should prepare a Return of all Charities
"connected with the Parish, and their annual values when be-
"queathed; also their annual value on the 25th of March, 1865;
"also a return of parish estates, how acquired, and their annual
"values at the dates of acquisition and March 1865, and how each
"have been appropriated, and that a copy be supplied to each
"Ratepayer prior to the following Vestry Meeting."

OFFICERS, &c. OF THE PARISH,

FOR THE YEAR 1867-8.

INCUMBENT.

THE REVEREND W. C. F. WEBBER 11, Charterhouse Square.

CHURCHWARDENS.

Mr. WILLIAM WALLFORD .... 159, Aldersgate Street.
" HENRY DIGBY .... 121, Aldersgate Street.

SIDESMEN.

Mr. GEORGE GODDARD .... 9, Carthusian Street.
" RICHARD HODGES LEIGH ...... 59, Barbican.
" JAMES KIRBY VICKERS .... 32, Aldersgate Street.
" JOSEPH WEST..................... 144, Aldersgate Street.

OVERSEERS.

Mr. JOHN LYNE....................... 61, Aldersgate Street.
" RICHARD RAYNER .... 142, Aldersgate Street.
" HENRY PIPER .... 21, Aldersgate Street.
" GEORGE MOWATT DICK ...... 112, Aldersgate Street.

GUARDIANS OF THE POOR.

Mr. JOHN SEWELL .... 65, Aldersgate Street.
" WILLIAM WALLFORD .... 159, Aldersgate Street.
" HENRY DIGBY .... 121, Aldersgate Street.

AUDITORS.

Mr. ROBERT JAMES CHAPLIN ...... 25, Aldersgate Street.
" EDWARD LANE .... 6, Aldersgate Street.
" WILLIAM MASTERS............... 13, Aldersgate Street.
" WILLIAM CAVE FOWLER ...... 16, Aldersgate Street.
" JOSEPH NICHOLAS GARROD... Falcon Street.

VESTRY CLERK & ASSISTANT OVERSEER.

Mr. JAMES R. CUTTS .... 11, Charterhouse Square, E.C.

TRUSTEES OF PARISH ESTATES

OF

St. Botolph without Aldersgate.

ROBERT BESLEY, Esq., Ald.	....	4, Fann Street.
Mr. THOMAS BLAKE	....	129, Aldersgate Street.
,, ROBERT JAMES CHAPLIN	......	25, Aldersgate Street.
,, JOHN ELDER DUFFIELD	......	68, Aldersgate Street.
,, CHARLES JAMES ELLETT	......	8, Jewin Street.
,, THOMAS HENRY ELLIS	....	51, Jewin Street.
,, THOMAS BLYVERS FLOYD	......	36, Aldersgate Street.
,, EDMUND FOX	....	75A, Little Britain.
,, JAMES BOOTE GOODINGE	......	21, Aldersgate Street.
,, JOHN BARNWELL HERRING	...	40, Aldersgate Street.
,, THOMAS ILLMAN	....	21, Little Britain.
,, EDWARD LANE	....	6, Aldersgate Street.
,, CHARLES MANN	....	159A, Aldersgate Street.
,, WILLIAM MASTERS	....	13, Aldersgate Street.
,, GEORGE MILLS	....	15, Goswell Street.
,, HENRY PIPER	....	21, Aldersgate Street.
,, JOHN SEWELL	....	65, Aldersgate Street.
,, GEORGE SIMS	....	147, Aldersgate Street.
,, WILLIAM WALLFORD	....	159, Aldersgate Street.

OBSERVATIONS.

The present Trust Deed is dated the 17th day of November, 1865, and vests the property of the Parish in the above-named Trustees, and gives the right to the Churchwardens to receive the rents, &c. &c.

The Trustees, Churchwardens, and Overseers have the exclusive power (subject to previous sanction of Vestry) to let or lease the house property of the Parish.

PARISH

OF

St. Botolph without Aldersgate.

A STATEMENT

OF

ALL CHARITIES

CONNECTED WITH THE PARISH,

AND

THEIR ANNUAL VALUE

WHEN BEQUEATHED, AND ON

25th MARCH, 1865.

DAME ANN PACKINGTON'S CHARITY.

WILL OF THE TESTATRIX,

As stated in the Report of the Master in Chancery of the 27th of November, 1827.

DAME ANN PACKINGTON, Widow, by her last Will and Testament, dated 24th of November, 1559, concerning the disposition of all those messuages, lands, and tenements, being customary and copyhold land, lying at Iselden, in the County of Middlesex, and holden by copy of court roll, of one of the prebendaries within the cathedral church of St. Paul's, in London, as of his manor and prebend of Iselden, that is to say, one messuage or tenement called the Crown, with the appurtenances, in Iselden aforesaid ; and one other messuage, with the appurtenances to the said messuage, called the Crown, adjoining, and 23 acres and 1 rood of land, in Iselden aforesaid, that is to say, 4 acres adjoining to the said messuage, and 15 acres and 1 rood, lying in the field called the Great Prebend Field, and 3 roods lying in the field purchased of one Robert Walker, one close called Little Colemans, containing by estimation $2\frac{1}{2}$ acres of land and 3 roods lying in a close called Great Colemans.

After reciting that she had surrendered the said messuages, lands, and premises, unto 20 persons therein named, to the use of her will, she willed and devised that the said trustees should, after her death, permit the master, wardens, and commonalty, of the freemen of the mystery of Clothworkers of the City of London, and their successors, to receive the rents and profits of the said messuages, lands, and premises, which at the then present time the said testatrix, by her will, stated to amount unto the yearly value of £16 16s. 9d. above all charges and expenses : and that the said master, wardens, and commonalty, after her decease should employ and bestow the said rents and profits yearly, for ever, in manner ensuing (that is to say)—that they shall distribute yearly among the poor people, being inhabitants within the parish of St. Dunstan's in the West of London, between the 1st day of November and the 1st day of February, the sum of £3 13s. 4d. in such form and proportions as the said master, wardens, and commonalty, should think necessary and convenient: and that they should distribute yearly among the poor people, inhabitants within the parish where she should be buried, £8 in form following, that is to say, towards finding of poor men's children of the same parish to school and learning the sum of £3, and other £3 thereof to be yearly distributed among the poor people of the same parish, between the 1st day of November and the 1st day of February, for ever. And that the said master, wardens, and commonalty, should yearly, on the 15th day of February, cause a learned man in the Scriptures of God to preach a sermon in the parish church of St. Dunstan's, and a like learned man to preach a sermon yearly within the parish church where she should be buried, on the day of the month that she should be buried; and that the said master, wardens, and commonalty, should on the same day distribute unto poor people in alms the sum of 40s. residue of the said sum of £8 and that they should give in reward under every such preacher the sum of 6s. 8d. over and above the said 40s. to be distributed to the poor, as aforesaid. And furthermore, that the said master, wardens, and commonalty, in consideration for their pains and trouble to be taken in and about the execution of the premises, and for and towards the payment of the fines, and for such surrenders as thereinafter mentioned, should have and retain yearly, so long as they should perform the contents of that her will, of the issues and profits of the said lands and premises the sum of £4 10s. 1d. And the said testatrix directed, that when the number of trustees seized of the said premises should be reduced to six, and no oftener, the premises should be surrendered to the use of twenty other persons, as trustees. And that if the said master, wardens, and commonalty, should not do in all things as she by her said will declared, after admonition in writing from the parson or vicar, and churchwardens, of the parish church where she should be buried, they should no further intermeddle with the profits of the said premises, but that her right heirs should receive and employ the same to the uses above declared; and if her right heirs should fail in their duty after a like admonition, the master and wardens of the fraternity of Merchant Tailors should have power to sell the said premises, for the best price, and distribute the same unto poor people in alms.

The said testatrix was buried in the parish of St. Botolph, Aldersgate.

DAME ANN PACKINGTON'S CHARITY.

Scheme for the Application of the Rents and Profits of the Charity Estate, as contained in the Master's Report of the 27th of November, 1827.

That the yearly rents and profits of the charity estates and funds shall in future be divided into sixteen parts, and be applied by the Clothworkers' Company in manner following:—

Four sixteenth parts thereof to be distributed yearly among the poor people being inhabitants within the Parish of St. Dunstan's, in the West of London, between the 1st day of November and the 1st day of February, in such form and proportions as the masters, wardens, and commonalty, of the said Company shall think necessary and convenient.

Eighth sixteenth parts thereof to be distributed yearly among the poor people, inhabitants within the Parish of St. Botolph Aldersgate, being the parish in which the said testatrix (Dame Ann Packington) was buried, in manner following, that is to say—three sixteenth parts towards *the finding of poor men's children of the same parish to school and learning.* Other three sixteenth parts to be yearly distributed among the poor people of the same parish, between the 1st day of November and the 1st day of February; and two sixteenth parts shall be distributed unto poor people in alms, by the said master, wardens, and commonalty, on such days as the sermons hereinafter mentioned shall be preached.

That the said Clothworkers' Company shall procure two sermons to be yearly preached on such days, and at such respective places, and by such preachers as the said testatrix hath by her will pointed out, and that the said Company shall pay to each of such preachers the sum of 21s. for each sermon.

And the other four sixteenth parts of such rents and profits, after payment for the sermons last mentioned, shall be retained by the master, wardens, and commonalty of the Clothworkers, for the use of the Company, in consideration of their pains and trouble to be taken in and about the execution of the premises, and for and towards the payment of the fines and surrenders, and the expenses incidentally attending the management of the estate, and the due distribution of the charity.

That in the distribution of the charity hereby directed preference shall in all cases be given to such persons as have never received parochial relief, or have been the longest without having received such relief.

That distinct accounts shall be kept of the receipt and expenditure on account of the charity; and such accounts be audited once a year, and when so audited, signed by the master and wardens of the Company.

That the estate belonging to the charity shall be distinguished and set out from the land belonging to the Clothworkers' Company by bound stones, 12-inches square, the same to be set down where the oak posts are now placed, such stones having proper marks thereon, and to be well sunk into the ground, leaving full twelve inches above ground, and to be afterwards kept in proper state and condition.

That the said charity estate shall be duly and properly managed, and let to the best advantage, under the superintendence of the said Clothworkers' Company, or their officers.

That a board or slab shall be put up in a public part of each of the churches of St. Dunstan's in the West, and St. Botolph *Aldersgate*, containing a short account of the said charity, so far as concerns such parishes respectively, with an explanation of its objects, and that the board or slab containing such inscribed account shall always be kept clean and in good repair.

DAME ANN PACKINGTON'S CHARITY.

Particulars of the Charity Estate and Property in Islington, Middlesex.
1850—1851.

	£ s. d.	£ s. d.	£ s. d.
No. 1—An old Brick Dwelling House and Garden, No. 1, Queen's Head Row, in the occupation of Cobbett, at an annual rent of			45 0 0
No. 2—A Brick Dwelling House and Garden, No. 2, Queen's Head Row, in the occupation of Rhodes, at an annual rent of			40 0 0
No. 3—A Brick Dwelling House and Garden, No. 3, Queen's Head Row, in the occupation of Bardoleau, at an annual rent of			45 0 0
No. 4—A Brick Dwelling House and Garden, No. 4, Queen's Head Row, in the occupation of Sinclair, at an annual rent of			45 0 0
No. 5—A Brick Dwelling House and Garden, No. 5, Queen's Head Row, in the occupation of Timewell, at an annual rent of		55 0 0	
Less for rent of Land belonging to Clothworkers' Company......		1 10 0	
			53 10 0
No. 6—A Plot of Ground, consisting of 1 acre, 1 rood, 11 perch, on Building Lease, to Henry Rydon for the term of years commencing at Midsummer, 1847, at an annual rent of			63 6 1
No. 7—Certain Land called the Crown Field and the Prebend Field, together with a Dwelling House, Stables, Barns, &c., leased to James Rhodes (on which he covenants to build 343 Houses) for 90 years, commencing at Michaelmas, 1846, at an annual rent of			800 0 0
			1091 16 1
5-16ths of which to be distributed to poor persons, inhabitants of Saint Botolph, Aldersgate	341 3 9		
3-16ths for finding poor men's children of Saint Botolph, Aldersgate, to school and learning	204 14 3½		
4-16ths to the Parish of St. Dunstan's in the West	272 19 0¼		
4-16ths to the Clothworkers' Company	272 19 0¼		1091 16 1

RENTAL OF PACKINGTON ESTATE,

From Christmas 1864 to Christmas 1865.

		£ s. d.	£ s. d.	£ s. d.
J. Rhodes				
,, (per Jay) 1 Yr's Rent to Xmas. 1865		10 0 0		
,, (per Vallance) ,, ,,		117 15 0		
			127 15 0	
,, (per Gardiner) ,, ,,			72 5 0	
J. Hebb ,, ,,			600 0 0	
				800 0 0
H. Rydon				
,, (per Robertson) ,, ,,			4 6 8	
,, (per Shum) ,, ,,			21 13 4	
,, (per Pye) ,, ,,			39 0 0	
				65 0 0
J. Hebb ,, ,,			25 0 0	
,, (per Cox) ,, ,,			20 0 0	
,, (per Waterman) ,, ,,			10 0 0	
H.M. Postmaster General ,, ,,			37 0 0	
J. Berry				
,, ½ yr's rent to Midsr. 1865	£11 0 0			
,, ¼ ,, to Christmas ,,	5 10 0			
		16 10 0		
H.M. Postmaster General				
¼ yr's rent to Christmas, 1865	5 10 0			
		22 0 0		
			114 0 0	
E. Barker 1 yr's rent ,, ,,			42 0 0	
			£1021 0 0	
1866 Aug. 25th By 2-16ths to be distributed to Poor after Sermon this day...............			127 12 6	
By 3-16ths finding poor men's Children to School....................			191 8 9	
Nov. 2nd By 3-16ths to be distributed by Churchwardens and Overseers to poor Housekeepers of the Parish between 1st November, 1866, and 1st February, 1867................			191 8 9	
8-16ths of Annual Rental			£510 10 0	

OBSERVATIONS.

At the date of the bequest the value of the Gift to this parish was **£8**, and at March 1865, according to the above rental, it was **£510 : 10 : 0** per annum.

It is distributed as above, viz.: **£319 : 1 : 3** *in money to the poor, and* **£191 : 8 : 9** *for finding poor men's children to Schools.*

STEPHEN SKYDMORE'S CHARITY.

Stephen Skydmore, by his will dated the 20th of March 1584, gave all his lands, tenements, and hereditaments situate within the precinct of the late dissolved priory called the Blackfriars, near Ludgate, in London, after the death of his wife, to the Vintners' Company of London, and their successors, to the intent that they should of and with the rents and profits of the said lands and premises, pay and perform the annuities and other things therein mentioned, that is to say, that the renter warden and one other officer of the said company, together with the Churchwardens or collectors for the poor of the following parishes, viz. 1. St. Anne's, Blackfriars, 2. St. Bride's, 3. St. Andrew's Holborn, 4. St. Sepulchre's, 5. St. Botolph's without Aldgate, 6. St. Botolph's without Aldersgate, 7. St. Giles's without Cripplegate, 8. St. Botolph's without Bishopsgate, 9. St. Leonard's Shoreditch, 10. St. Mary Matfellon in Whitechapel, 11. St. Giles's Southwark, 12. St. Katherine's Hospital by the Tower of London, 13. St. Saviour in Bermondsey-street, commonly called St. Mary Magdalen, 14. St. George's Southwark, 15. St. Mary Avery's beyond the Water, 16. St. Giles's in the Fields, and 17, St. James's Clerkenwell, should distribute, and pay among the poor people of each of the said parishes yearly, the sum of 20s. in wood, coal, or other fuel, in the month of October; and he also willed that the said company should, of the said rents and profits, pay yearly to the Churchwardens of the parish of St. Stephen Coleman-street, the sum of 52s. to the intent they should every Sunday in the year, bestow one dozen of bread among twelve of the poorest people of the said parish, after morning prayers in the parish church.

He also directed the said company to pay out of the rents and profits of the said lands, 20s. a year in money, wood or coal, among the poorest persons of the said company, and further charged the said lands with a payment of £24 per annum to the city of Cork. The premises charged with these payments, consist now of 17 freehold houses, situate in and near the Broadway in the parish of St. Anne Blackfriars, and produce rents amounting in the aggregate to £315 per annum.

The several annual sums given by the will, are paid by the company, to the parish officers of the respective parishes, the officers of the company not interfering in the distribution.

OBSERVATIONS.

The yearly sum of £1 is regularly received from the Renter Warden of the Vintners' Company, and distributed in bread to the poor.

TAMWORTH GIFT.

CHRISTOPHER TAMWORTH, Esquire, by his Will bearing date 28th April 1624, and proved in the Prerogative Court of Canterbury, directed that his executors thereinafter named should deliver into the hands of the Dean and Prebend of the College of St. Peter, of the City of Westminster, 400 marks to the intent that they might therewith cause 20 marks of land of inheritance of yearly rent to be purchased with the consent of his executors and the parishioners of the Parish of St. Botolphus without Aldersgate, whereby there might be one in Holy Orders maintained to say such divine service as the Church of England should allow of every working day in the year twice, viz. at or about nine o'clock in the morning, and at or about three o'clock in the afternoon, in the parish church of St. Botolphus aforesaid; and he declared that if the curate of the said church would undertake it, he would be a fit man; but if he it did not daily, duly, orderly, and reverently, and at or about the times prefixed, and of right, and in regard of this pension only of all others, he would not have him nor any of his successors to have it, for that his meaning was not to augment the curate's wages, but to have divine service said there to the honour and glory of God; and he further declared that his meaning was, that the Dean and Prebend aforesaid, with the consent of the said parishioners, should for ever appoint a fit person to say divine service as aforesaid; and that the parishioners of right should claim and challenge, in regard of that annual pension and stipend, to have divine service said accordingly, and that if there should be default upon complaint by the said parishioners to the Lord Chancellor of England, or the Lord Keeper of the Great Seal of England for the time being, that the Lord Chancellor or Lord Keeper should take order that the land intended to be purchased should be employed for the uses aforesaid, and not to any other use whatsoever.

The testator also directed his executors to deliver £100 more into the hands of the said Dean and Prebend to the end that they should see £20 of land of annual revenue of inheritance bought with it to allow perpetually to six poor men past labour, dwelling and inhabiting within the parish of St. Botolph aforesaid, 40s. every year a-piece during their lives, and to four poor widows likewise past labour, so long as they should continue widows, dwelling in the said parish, 40s. a-piece every year during their lives, with this limitation, that both the six poor men and the four poor widows should be bound to repair every working day in the year, twice, to hear divine service in the said parish church at the hours and times before prefixed; and he directed that if any of the said poor men or widows should refuse, or voluntarily neglect, without just cause, to come to the said church to hear divine service all the time of divine service, others should be chosen in their place by the discretion of the curate of the said parish, the churchwardens, and the constables for the time being, and six of the principal parishioners named for that purpose by the residue of the parishioners; and that the said poor men and widows should have their pensions paid them quarterly, and he further directed that all the lands so to be purchased should be continually in the hands of ten feoffees at the least, to the uses aforesaid, being all freeholders in the said parish, or persons of good account and dwelling in the said parish; and that upon every new feoffment the number of twenty-four or thirty persons should be feoffees.

The several sums bequeathed by Christopher Tamworth for the benefit of a minister who should read divine service in the parish church twice every day, and of poor persons who should attend thereat, appear to have been laid out in the purchase of an estate in Vang and other places in the county of Essex. This estate was however sold; and by indenture bearing date 17th August 1658 between James Flesher and twenty-four others, parishioners of St. Botolph of the one part, and the Rev. George Maule of the other part, the said James Flesher and others, by the order and with the consent of the parishioners of St. Botolph assembled in vestry to treat of the affairs of that parish in consideration of £470 conveyed to the said George Maule and his heirs, the said estate, by the description of a messuage or farm, commonly called Lunses, alias Moyses or Colehams, with all the lands &c. thereto belonging, containing by estimation 152 acres, and situate in the parishes of Fang, alias Vang, Pitsey, Bartlesden, and Novingdon, or some or one of them in the county of Essex, and the said James Flesher and others covenanted that the said premises should be for ever freed and discharged from the payment of the several yearly sums of 20 marks and £20, and all other charitable uses limited or appointed by Christopher Tamworth, Esq., deceased, by his Will of the date above mentioned.

By indenture bearing date 30th April 1658 between Edward Fust and others, executors of Edmund Denton deceased of the one part, and James Flesher and twenty-four others, parishioners of St. Botolph without Aldersgate, of the other part, reciting that the Dean and Chapter of St. Peter Westminster, late parson of the parish of St. Botolph aforesaid, and Thomas Smith and another, churchwardens of the said parish, had, by indenture bearing date 18th December, Charles II., demised to Sir Henry Martin, for the term of 60 years from Lady Day then next, under the yearly rent of £1 13s. 8d., a tenement with the cellars and a court yard some time a garden thereto adjoining, with the appurtenances called the church house, situate in Aldersgate Street, adjoining to the sign of the Peacock, there and further reciting that the warden and scholars of New College, Oxford, by indenture bearing date 19th July, 14th Charles, demised to the said Sir Henry Martin, for the term of 40 years from Lady Day then last at the yearly rent of £8, nine messuages, cottages, or tenements, with the garden, yards, and buildings then newly erected by the said Sir Henry Martin, lying in Petty Wales or elsewhere in the parish of Great St. Bartholomew, near West Smithfield, and further reciting that the interest in the said several indentures had become vested in the said Edmund Denton; and further reciting that by indenture bearing date 11th July 1655, reciting that part of the staircase and larder of the great messuage in Aldersgate Street, whereof the said Edmund Denton was then possessed, with the cellar under and terrett over the said larder, was erected on part of the lands belonging to St. Bartholomew's Hospital, being formerly part of their Inn called the Peacock, and that the mayor, commonalty, and citizens of London, governors of the said hospital, had demised the said Inn to William Millett for a certain term ; the said William Millett demised to the said Edmund Denton the parcel of of land whereon the said staircase, &c. had been built, for the term of 20 years from Lady Day then last at the yearly rent of 20s.; the said Edward Fust and others, executors of the said Edmund Denton, in consideration of £760 paid by the churchwardens and parishioners of St. Botolph aforesaid (as well for the purchase of the premises before mentioned as for a stable and coach-house with the waste grounds whereon the same stood which had been sold by the said executors to the said parishioners) and by the direction of the parishioners assembled in vestry conveyed to the said James Flesher and others, their executors, &c., the said premises for the residue of the said terms of years upon trust, that they should, with so much of the surplusage of the rents and profits thereof (above the rents reserved by the said leases) as should be necessary during the continuance of the said leases, support, maintain, and perform the charitable uses trusts and purposes relating to the said church and parish of St. Botolph, and the minister and poor there limited and appointed by the last Will of Christopher Tamworth, Esquire bearing date 28th April 1624; part of the purchase money before mentioned, viz. £460 being raised by the sale of a farm in or about Vang in Essex, formerly bought with the money given by the said Christopher Tamworth for the maintenance of the said charitable use, which farm the said parishioners were forced to sell in regard the same was so decayed that it would not yield above £20 per annum; and upon further trust to suffer the churchwardens for the time being to receive and dispose of the residue of the rents to such uses as the said parishioners should appoint.

The premises described in the preceding indenture as the Church house, with the appurtenances, appear to have been vested in the Dean and Chapter of Westminster, the rectors of this parish, and the churchwardens, prior to the passing of the statute for the dissolution of chantries, and they were afterwards granted out by the Crown to Edmund Duffield and John Babington, who conveyed the same to William Wilford and Nicholas Wilson, and by indenture bearing date 1st November 1658, John Wilford, son and heir of William Wilford who was the survivor, conveyed the same to James Flesher and others parishioners of St. Botolph, upon trust to demise the premises in such manner as the parishioners in vestry should appoint, and to permit the churchwardens to receive the rents for such charitable uses and purposes as the same had been usually disposed of and employed by the said parishioners in and about the repairs of the said church, the relief of the poor, and other the public affairs of the said parish.

These and all other the premises mentioned in the indenture of 30th April 1658, except the leasehold premises held under the warden and scholars of New College, have been conveyed to new feoffees from time to time upon the like trusts as declared in the indenture of 1st November 1658.

The premises held under lease from the warden and scholars of New College have been demised from time to time at the expiration of every 14 years for similar terms of 40 years. The present lease was granted in the year 1828 to the same persons as are feoffees for the other property.

From these documents it appears that the sum of £470, the consideration for the sale of the estate in Essex, which was purchased with the bequest of Christopher Tamworth, was laid out by the parishioners, with other money, in obtaining the immediate possession of certain premises to the reversion of which they were previously entitled, and the payment of the two yearly sums of £20 and £13 6s. 8d., in respect of Tamworth's charity, has been considered as charged upon these premises, (part of which formed the site of the old parish workhouse) the residue of the rents and profits being applicable according to the trusts declared in 1658 for the general use of the parish.

OBSERVATIONS.

This Charity is distributed as follows, viz. :—There is paid to the minister the sum of **£13 6s. 8d.** *for Divine Service, and* **10s.** *a quarter to each of 10 poor and aged persons called prayer people, namely, six men and four women for attending prayers at the parish Church. These pensioners are appointed from time to time, as vacancies occur, in manner following :—*

Notice is given on the church of the vacancy, and a meeting is appointed to be held on the following Sunday, after morning service, of the electors under the Will of Christopher Tamworth, for the purpose of electing a man or woman, as the case may require, to fill the vacancy, such person not receiving regularly weekly allowance from the poor's rate.

MORLEY'S CHARITY.

In a book called "The Record Book," containing copies of the documents relating to the greater number of charities for this parish, there are entered copies of the following documents relating to the charity of John Morley, viz.: a Deed bearing date the 20th January 1588, whereby the Company of Goldsmiths granted a rent charge of £5 out of a messuage in Foster Lane to John Sotherton and his heirs; also a testamentary paper bearing date 24th January 1588, whereby the said John Sotherton devised the said rent charge to the parson and churchwardens of St. Botolph and their successors; and also a deed of covenant bearing date 29th January 1588, whereby the parson and churchwardens of the parish of St. Botolph covenanted with Edward Caryll and Elizabeth his wife, late wife of John Morley, that they would yearly pay weekly, upon every Sunday throughout the year, in the parish church, five groats to five poor men, inhabitants of St. Botolph, of the most aged and impotent, one groat to each, which would amount to £4 6s. 8d., and also that the said churchwardens would cause a sermon to be preached on the Feast of St. John the Baptist, in remembrance of the donor, and that they would pay to the preacher 6s. 8d. for the sermon, and that of the other 6s. 8d. one moiety should be given to the churchwardens, and the other to the parish clerk. And it was agreed that the five poor men should be inhabitants within the parish, and be nominated by the churchwardens, and more part of the discreet, substantialest, and honest parishioners at a vestry or otherwise at their discretion.

OBSERVATIONS.

The yearly sum of **£5** *is paid to the churchwardens by the clerk of the Goldsmiths' Company, out of which* **6s. 8d.** *is paid to the minister, and* **3s. 4d.** *to the parish clerk; the churchwardens, though in fact they have never taken it, are entitled to the further sum of* **3s. 4d.**, *leaving* **£4 6s. 8d.**, *applicable to the poor, which is distributed in Bread.*

GADBURY'S CHARITY.

Richard Gadbury, by his Will bearing date the 10th August 1624 as entered in the record book above mentioned, gave his house and land at Eyworth, in the county of Bedford, to Edmund Anderson and his heirs upon condition that he should pay amongst other things the yearly sum of £4 6s. 8d. in the parish church of St. Botolph to the deputy of the ward and the two churchwardens of the said parish, by two payments, one on the Feast of St. Thomas the Apostle, and the other 1st May, and directed that the same deputy and churchwardens, with the minister of the said parish, should see the same bestowed as follows, viz.: that he should have two sermons preached yearly in the parish church, one on the 26th May, and the other on the 1st January, and that the preacher receive 10s. each time, and that he should give to thirty poor people of the said parish, fifteen men and fifteen women, 1s. each half yearly on the days aforesaid, immediately after the sermon, to the clerk of the parish 2s., and to the sexton for tolling the bell 1s. 4d. each time.

OBSERVATIONS.

The yearly sum of **£4 6s. 10d.** *is received from the Charity Commissioners for England, being the dividends on* **£144 14s. 6d.** *consols, and is applied as follows, viz.:—the sum of* **£1** *to the minister, though in fact no sermon is preached on either of the days appointed, and* **4s.** *and* **2s. 8d.** *to the clerk and sexton, and the residue* **£3 : 0s. 2d.** *is distributed in Bread to the poor.*

TAYLOR'S CHARITY.

In the record book before mentioned, there is entered a copy of an Indenture bearing date 15th June 1616, between Roger Taylor of the one part, and Edward Topsell then the minister of the parish church of St. Botolph without Aldersgate, and Matthias Kempster and Christopher Walton, churchwardens, of the other part; whereby the said Roger Taylor granted to the said minister and churchwardens, and their successors, an annuity of £5, payable out of the mansion house of the granter in Aldersgate Street, in the parish of St. Botolph, yearly, upon Ash Wednesday for ever; and he gave the said minister and churchwardens power to distrain if the same should be in arrear for fourteen days, with power of re-entry in case of non-payment for twenty-eight days, and the said minister and churchwardens covenanted with the said Roger Taylor that every year, on Maunday Thursday, there should be a sermon preached in the parish church in the forenoon, and that they and their successors would then and there distribute the said £5 in manner following, viz. :

	£	s.	d.
To the preacher	0	7	0
Clerk and sexton	0	3	0
To sixty poor people, men and women, inhabiting within the said parish, viz. to twenty of the most needy 2s. each, and to the other forty 1s. each	4	0	0
To the parish minister and churchwardens for their pains, if they be present and see this charity performed, 2s. a piece	0	6	0
And to such poor people as they should think fit	0	4	0
	£5	0	0

And it was provided that in case the said minister and churchwardens, or their successors, should neglect the observance of the said sermon, and the distribution of the £5 on Maunday Thursday as above, (if they could have the said £5 to discharge the same withal,) then the grant of the said annuity should be void.

OBSERVATIONS.

The yearly sum of **£5** *is received from the Goldsmiths' Company who are possessed of several houses in Aldersgate Street, of which probably the premises charged with this payment form part.*

This sum is distributed as follows: Minister for sermon **7s.**, *parish clerk* **1s. 6d.**, *sexton* **1s. 6d.**, *and the balance* **£4 10s. 0d.** *is distributed in bread to the poor.*

NORMANSED CHARITY.

In a list of the benefactions to the poor entered in the record book before mentioned, it is stated that Richard Normansed, in 1694, gave to the poor of this parish the yearly sum of £5, and in a small book containing an account of the benefactions which has been copied from older books of the same description, it is added that this annuity is to be applied towards the relief of poor decayed housekeepers of this parish at Michaelmas and Lady-day yearly, and that the donor charged his estate in Cross Key Court, Little Britain, with the payment thereof.

OBSERVATIONS.

The yearly sum of £5 is now paid to the churchwardens as follows: £2 10s. part thereof by Mr. Doudney, and £2 10s., less income tax, by Mr. Phillips, being the rent charge on the several houses in Cross Key Court, Little Britain, mentioned in the Will of the donor.

This amount is also distributed in bread to the poor.

SNOW'S CHARITY.

Thomas Snow, by his Will bearing date 2nd May 1651, as entered in the record book before mentioned, directed that his brother Samuel and his heirs should pay yearly out of his messuages in Fann's Alley to the churchwardens or other officers of St. Botolph without Aldersgate, £4 by quarterly payments, to be distributed by the said churchwardens or other officers in bread among poor people inhabiting the said parish, weekly, viz. every Sunday one dozen and a half of bread, and if any part of the said £4 should remain at the year's end, he directed the same to be distributed in bread on Easter day amongst the poor.

OBSERVATIONS.

This yearly sum of £4, less income tax, is received from the assignees of Mrs. Charlotte Dimsdale, in respect of the premises in Fann's Alley charged therewith, and the balance is distributed in bread to the poor.

WARD'S CHARITY.

In the record book before mentioned it is stated that Mrs. Ward, in 1660, gave £60 to the minister and churchwardens to settle £3 yearly for ever, to be paid on Good Friday, namely, to the poor £2, to the minister £1, and it is added that the parishioners agreed to secure the payment thereof out of the rents of their houses in Black Horse Alley.

The feoffees of the parish have some houses in Black Horse Alley, out of the rents of which £1 per annum is paid to the minister, and the residue is to be considered as charged with the yearly sum of £2 for the poor.

OBSERVATIONS.

The above sum of £3 appears to be regularly received, and out of which £1 is paid to the minister, and the remaining £2 is distributed in bread to the poor at the parish church on Sundays.

PEASE'S CHARITY.

In a small book containing an account of the benefactions to the parish, it is stated that William Pease, by Will bearing date 23rd of December 1682, charged his lands at Harrow, or Pinner, in the county of Middlesex, during the residue of a term of 1500 years, granted in the reign of Edward VI., with the payment of an annuity of £2 12s. to the churchwardens of this parish, to be by them and their successors laid out yearly in good and sound bread for the relief of the poor of the said parish at the rate of 12d. a week weekly.

OBSERVATIONS.

The churchwardens receive the above mentioned sum of £2 12s. annually from the Sadlers' Company, on the Wednesday after Lady Day, and the same distributed in bread to the poor.

CRIPPES' CHARITY.

ROBERT CRIPPES, by his Will bearing date 1st February 1576, gave to the poor people of the parish of St. Botolph Aldersgate 20s., to be distributed amongst them at the discretion of his executors and the overseers, else at the discretion of the master and wardens of the Brewers' Company, to be payable out of his messuages on the west side of Aldersgate, in the parish of St. Botolph.

By a Decree of Commissioners of Charitable uses, bearing date 20th July, 32 Charles I., it was ordered that certain premises theretofore called or known by the sign of the Seven Stars in Aldersgate Street, then divided into several tenements, should stand charged with the payment of the said annuity at the Feast of the Annunciation yearly to the churchwardens of the parish of St. Botolph for the time being.

OBSERVATIONS.

The sum of £1 is paid yearly by the Trustees of the late Thomas Loveland, the owner of several houses on the west side of Aldersgate Street, and the amount is distributed in bread to the poor.

ADAMS'S CHARITY.

By Indenture dated 20th July 1582, and made between Richard Adams and Margaret his wife of the one part, and Richard Brown and Elizabeth his wife of the other part, it was covenanted between the parties that the possessors of the premises therein mentioned, after the decease of Richard and Margaret Adams, should pay yearly to the churchwardens of St. Anne and Agnes near Aldersgate, St. Botolph without Aldersgate, and St. Michael Bassishaw, in London, 30s., to be distributed to the poor of the said parishes, that is to say, 10s. to each parish.

The premises mentioned in the deed are a messuage at Boyden's Hill, in the parish of Aldenham in Hertfordshire, and a messuage with a garden or orchard at Crancott Hill in the same parish; they are now the property of Mrs. Sarah Noyes.

OBSERVATIONS.

The above mentioned charity does not appear to have been received since the year 1853.

CONYER'S CHARITY.

The following abstracts are taken from the Record Book which contains copies of the documents relating to the greater number of charities of this parish. By Indenture, bearing date 11th April 1592, the master, wardens, and assistants of the Company of Merchant Tailors, in consideration of £100 of the money of John Conyers, granted to John Sotherton, one of the barons of the Exchequer, his heirs and assigns, a yearly rent charge of £5, issuing out of their great messuage and tenement thereto adjoining with the appurtenances in Aldermanbury, on the east side of the same, in the parish of our Lady Aldermanbury, payable at the four usual feasts, with a power of entry and distress in case of nonpayment. The said John Sotherton, by a testamentary writing bearing date 10th of May 1592, gave the said yearly rent charge of £5 to the parson and churchwardens of the parish church of St. Botolph without Aldersgate; and by Indenture bearing date 11th May 1592, the parson and churchwardens of St. Botolph without Aldersgate covenanted with the said John Conyers that the churchwardens of the said parish and their successors would yearly distribute the amount of the said rent charge in manner following, viz. weekly, on every Sunday throughout the whole year, in the parish church of St. Botolph, as of the free gift and alms of the said John Conyers in the sum of five groats amongst five of the poorest and neediest men and women being inhabitants within the parish, and the most aged and impotent men of the said parish, to every of them one groat immediately after morning or evening prayer, which would amount yearly to the sum of £4 6s. 8d. And also that the said churchwardens and their successors would yearly cause a sermon to be preached by some godly learned and discreet preacher, in remembrance of the donor, on Rogation Sunday, in the said parish church, and would pay to him upon the finishing of every such sermon the sum of 6s. 8d., and that they would distribute the remaining 6s. 8d., one moiety thereof to the churchwardens, and the other to the parish clerk, for their pains in the receipt and distributing the said money, and warning the poor men from time to time that should receive the same; the said poor men and women to be nominated, from time to time, by the said churchwardens and the more part of the discreet, substantialest, and honest parishioners at a vestry or otherwise at their discretion.

OBSERVATIONS.

The Merchant Tailors' Company are in possession of an inn in Aldermanbury, called the George, which is supposed to be the property charged with the annuity of **£5**.

The yearly sum of **£4** *(***£1** *being deducted for land tax) is received from the Company by the churchwardens, out of which is paid to the minister for preaching a sermon on Rogation Sunday* **6s. 8d.**, *and* **3s. 4d.** *to the parish clerk.*

The churchwardens are also entitled to the sum of **3s. 4d.**, *but they do not receive it; the balance* **£3 10s.** *is distributed in bread to the poor.*

DAWTREY'S CHARITY.

By Indenture bearing date 6th January 1631, as appears from the Record Book before mentioned, between Thomas Smith of the one part, and Sir Henry Martin, Sir Richard Sutton, and twenty-two other parishioners or inhabitants within the parish of St. Botolph, of the other part, reciting that   Dawtrey of her charitable disposition towards the poor of St. Botolph, wherein she had spent some part of her time, did, in her lifetime, declare her desire that her son Henry Dawtrey should distribute some part of her estate for the relief of the poor of the same and other parishes, and that the said Henry Dawtrey had paid to the churchwardens £20 in performance of his mother's desire, and £5 more as his own gift, to the intent that a rent charge might be purchased therewith; the said Thomas Smith, in consideration of the said sum of £25, granted to the parties of the second part a rent charge of 26s., payable yearly at Lady-day out of a messuage then called the Golden Ball, in Aldersgate Street, within the parish of St. Botolph, with a power of distress and entry in case of non-payment.

OBSERVATIONS.

The rent charge of **£1 6s.** *less income tax, is paid regularly at the office of the Chamberlain of the City of London, who probably became liable to this payment by purchasing the house charged therewith for the enlargement of Aldersgate Street.*

This sum is also distributed in bread to the poor.

MARGARET DANE'S CHARITY.

Mrs. Margaret Dane, by will dated 16th May 1579, gave to the Master, Wardens and Company of Ironmongers of London, £2,000 on condition that the said Master and Wardens, with six other of the substantiallest of the said Company, should pay to twenty young men, free of the Company of Ironmongers of honest name and fame, and inhabitants of the City of London, or its suburbs, (always retailers of linen cloth to be preferred before others,) to be appointed by the said Master, Wardens and six others of the said Company, the said sum of £2,000, that is to say, £100 to each of the said poor young men, to have the same for three years, upon finding sureties to the Master, Wardens, and other six before mentioned, for the repayment thereof, at the end of the said three years, to the intent, that the said sum of £2,000 should then be delivered to twenty other poor young men of the same Company on like conditions, and so on for three years to three years. And she directed that the said Company should, in consideration of the benefit of the said £2,000, pay in legacies the sum of £100 yearly for ever, that is to say, to Christ's Hospital, Saint Bartholomew's Hospital, and Saint Thomas's Hospital in Southwark, to each of them ten pounds the piece, amounteth to thirty pounds; to be paid unto each of them five pounds every half-year for ever. Also I will that the said Company shall pay ten pounds yearly for ever, to be distributed at their discretion to twenty poor maids within every year of the days of their marriage. Also I will that they pay ten pounds yearly for ever to the Universities of Oxford and Cambridge, to pay to each five pounds for the relief and bringing up in learning two poor scholars, the one to be in Oxford and the other in Cambridge. The Houses in which they shall be brought up to be named at the discretion of my executors. And I will that the said money shall come amongst all the poor scholars of the said houses; that he that hath it the one year shall not have the next again, but to come through the whole number of the poor, and then to revert again orderly. Furthermore, I will that the said Company of Ironmongers shall employ in Bread and Beef, to be bought at the best hand, every year for ever, the sum of ten pounds, the same to be distributed and divided at the discretion of the Master and Wardens of the said Company amongst the prisoners in the houses hereafter named—that is to say, Newgate, Ludgate, the two Compters, the Queen Bench, the Marshallsea, The White Lyon in Southwark, and the Convict House at Westminster. Furthermore, I will that the said Company shall pay five pounds a year, to be paid twenty-five shillings every quarter of a year yearly for ever towards the maintenance of a School, to be erected at Bishop Storford, and if it so chance that the said School go not forward (as God forbid), then I will that the said five pounds be distributed quarterly to the poor people for the same parish for ever. Also, I will that the said Company shall provide and buy for the poorest people of the twenty-four Wards in London, at the best hand, twelve thousand of faggotts every year for ever, the same to be distributed to each Ward, part and part alike, at the discretion of the Master and Wardens of the said Company, at two several times of the year—that is to say, the one half at Christmas and the other half at Hallowtide. Moreover, I will that the said Company of Ironmongers shall yearly for ever bestow ten pounds upon a dinner to be made at their Hall the same day as it shall please God to call me out of this transitory life, at which dinner I will that their Company be assembled according to their accustomed order at other their feasts, provided always that if the said Company of Ironmongers shall refuse, or neglect to put in sufficient sureties for the said two thousand pounds, and the performance of all the legacies herein by me enjoined them, to pay in the consideration of the said two thousand pounds according to this my last will and testament, then my mind and will is, that they shall not have the said two thousand pounds, but that the said two thousand pounds be paid to the Company of Mercers, &c. &c.

The following is the earliest entry in the account books of the Company respecting this part of Mrs. Dane's Gift.

"1604 To the bequest of Mrs. Dane,

"Imprimis paid and delivered, the Alderman's deputies of the "twenty-four Wards in London, to be by their oversight and "direction, with the aid of the Overseers for the poor in the said "several Wards, bestowed in fagots, distributed to the poor people "in the said Ward, £25; which, to knowledge of their accounting, "was carefully preserved according to the Donor's intent.

OBSERVATIONS.

The original value of the Gift was £1. 0s. 10d. to each Ward, which were divided equally among the different Parishes in each Ward, but a great portion of the funds having been lost, the present income of the Charity is about £45, and the bequests are accordingly paid in proportion. The amount paid to each Ward is now about 10s.

The Gift being to the Ward, the sum of between **4s. and 5s.** *only per annum is received from the Company of Ironmongers by the Churchwardens of the Parish, and distributed in Bread to the Poor.*

ALDERMAN SMITH'S GIFT.

Henry Smith, a Citizen and Alderman of London, by Deeds dated 20th October, 1620, did convey and assure unto Trustees for Charitable Purposes, all his real and personal Estates, but afterwards being desirous that the disposition of his property might be settled after his death, he exhibited his Bill in Chancery, and the following Decree, dated 20th June, 1626, was made thereon, which fully set forth the Deeds, with their Trusts, &c. and is as follows, viz :—

DECREE.

Whereas the said plaintiff being charitably minded and disposed did in October 1620 by deed convey and assure to the said Earl of Essex Richard late Earl of Dorset deceased Sir Edward Francis now also deceased Mr. Serjeant Amhurst John Middleton William Wingfield and George Whitmore and their heirs the manor of Warbleton and the farms of South Wick and Iwood with the lands thereunto belonging in the county of Sussex and divers other lands tenements and hereditaments of a good yearly value and by another deed of the same date did also grant to the said Mr. Serjeant Amhurst George Whitmore John Middleton and William Wingfield all his the said plaintiff's ready money except one hundred pounds and all his personal estate goods and chattels whatsoever But each of the said deeds did contain a power of revocation at his will and pleasure at any time after during his natural life and by another deed of the same date did declare that the said several deeds and conveyances of the said manors and personal estate were made upon this special trust and confidence that the said plaintiff Henry Smith should receive out of the profits of the said premises yearly the sum of five hundred pounds for and towards his maintenance and that the said parties trusted should dispose of the residue of the profits of the said premises and of the said personal estate in such sort and to such charitable uses as the said plaintiff by his last will and testament in writing to be by him sealed at any time during his natural life should nominate limit and appoint and in default of such nomination limitation or appointment then to such charitable uses as the said Earls of Essex and Dorset Sir Edward Francis George Whitmore Serjeant Amhurst John Middleton and William Wingfield their heirs or assigns should think fit And whereas the said Sir Edward Francis was at the time of the making and sealing of the said several deeds indebted to the plaintiff in the sum of three thousand pounds and the said John Middleton was also indebted to the said plaintiff in the sum of four thousand pounds or thereabouts to be forthwith cleared and perfected by account and the said Sir Richard Lumley was then also indebted to the said plaintiff in the sum of one thousand pounds and the said Mr. Serjeant Amhurst was also indebted to the said plaintiff in the sum of one thousand pounds most of which debts were in strictness of law contrary to the true intent and meaning of all the said parties released and discharged by the said deeds and a deed thereafter mentioned And whereas also the said plaintiff continuing his charitable intention on the 12th day of June 1625 for some reasons and persuasions him moving by other deeds of the same date did release the said several powers of revocation in the former conveyances mentioned and by another deed of the same date made between the plaintiff of the one part and the said Earl of Essex Mr. Justice Crook Sir Christopher Nevill the said Sir Richard Lumley Mr. Serjeant Amhurst John Middleton William Wingfield Sir Edward Francis deceased and George Lowe William Blake William Rolfe and Richard Gurnet defendants in this suit of the other part did declare his intention and meaning to be that the rents issues and profits of the said manors and premises together with the said personal estate should be employed and bestowed by them the said Earl and other the defendants last named and their heirs for and towards the relief of poor prisoners hurt and maimed soldiers poor maids' marriages setting up of poor apprentices amending of highways losses sustained by fire or shipwreck or otherwise to or for such charitable uses as they the said parties trusted or any seven or more of them their heirs or assigns should from time to time think most meet and convenient notwithstanding which said last deed the said plaintiff for that all the said estate did move from him and did proceed merely from his pious and charitable intention in which respect he did still desire that he himself during his life might have the employment and disposition thereof and that he might declare limit and appoint to what good and charitable uses and how and in what manner the same should be employed or disposed either in his life-time or after his death and in case no such declaration should be made by him while he lived then to the end to have the same more surely performed after his death he much desired that the disposition thereof might be settled in such sort as is hereafter expressed and for the better effecting thereof did exhibit his bill into this Court against the said defendants who did all make their answers thereunto wherein they have confessed that the said several deeds and conveyances were freely and voluntarily made by the said plaintiff of his own mere motion without any valuable consideration at all and they the said Sir Edward Francis Sir Richard Lumley John Middleton and Serjeant Amhurst did also confess that they were and are respectively indebted to the said plaintiff in the several sums before mentioned and did all of them submit to the order of this Honourable Court both concerning the said manors lands and personal estate and also concerning the payment or securing of the said debts Whereupon the truth of the said cause appearing to be as aforesaid it is this present day upon hearing counsel on all sides and by and with the free and voluntary assent of the said Serjeant Amhurst and John Middleton now present in Court and by and with the full consent of the counsel of the rest of the defendants ordered adjudged and decreed that the estate and interest of the said manors and lands and also of the said personal estate shall forthwith by good and sufficient conveyance and assurance in the law be settled and vested by such of the said defendants in whom the interest thereof doth now remain in and upon the said Earl of Essex Mr. Justice Crooke Sir Christopher Nevill Sir Richard Lumley William Wingfield George Lowe William Blake William Rolfe and Richard Gurnet and in such others as the said plaintiff shall nominate and appoint upon trust and confidence that they the said parties trusted and their heirs shall permit and suffer the said plaintiff to have the use of his mansion-house in Silver-street London for and during the term of his life and upon this further trust and confidence that the said parties trusted and to be trusted shall suffer the said plaintiff and his assigns during his natural life to receive the rents issues and profits of the said manors lands leases and personal estate and the interest of his money and to dispose of the said rents interest and personal estate for his own maintenance and for and towards such charitable uses and otherwise for the benefit and relief of his kindred as he the said plaintiff shall think

fit to nominate and appoint and to this further intent and
purpose and upon this further trust and confidence that they
the said parties trusted or to be trusted or seven of them
at the least and their heirs and assigns shall after the death of
the said plaintiff employ bestow and dispose of the rents issues and
profits of the said manors and lands and of the said personal estate
not disposed of by the said plaintiff in his life-time to and for the
charitable uses aforesaid and to and for the purchasing and restoring
to the Church of impropriations for the maintenance of learned godly
preachers and to and for such other charitable uses as the said plaintiff
by his last will and testament in writing or by any writing to be by
him sealed and delivered in the presence of three witnesses or more
shall nominate declare limit or appoint or in default thereof to such
charitable uses as shall be declared limited or appointed by the said
persons trusted or to be trusted or any seven of them And it is further
ordered and decreed that in the said new conveyance to be made
provision shall be that whensoever so many of the said parties trusted
shall die as that the number of them that shall survive shall not exceed six that then the said six or the survivors of them shall make a
new conveyance and settle the said manors lands and personal estate
upon themselves and so many more to be nominated by the Lord
Archbishop of Canterbury and Lord Chancellor or Lord Keeper of
the Great Seal for the time being as shall make up the full number
of thirteen at the least to the intents and purposes aforesaid And it
is further ordered and decreed by and with the like assent of the said
Richard Amhurst John Middleton and Sir Richard Lumley that the
said John Middleton Serjeant Amhurst and Sir Richard Lumley shall
well and truly pay or sufficiently secure the said several debts by
them severally and respectively owing as aforesaid to the said feoffees
the same security to be by mortgage of land or sufficient securities in
such sort as Mr. Justice Crooke shall think fit on or before the feast
of St. Bartholomew the Apostle then next coming to be paid in with
interest to the said plaintiff at reasonable days to be appointed by the
plaintiff for that purpose And lastly it is ordered and decreed that the
deeds evidences and writings concerning the said manors and lands
and personal estate shall forthwith be brought into this Court by such
of the defendants as have the same to the intent that the same may there
remain in safety to be further disposed of as this Court shall think fit

And this Court doth declare that the said Richard Amhurst and John Middleton who have assented to this decree have therein and all things else appearing to this Court behaved themselves justly and uprightly and especially in that they have so freely and willingly condescended to the securing of the said debts which were in law discharged for which cause this Court doth not only free them of blame but esteem them worthy of commendation and therefore this Court doth wish the said Mr. Smith to esteem of them accordingly.

The Deed by which divers Estates are settled to Charitable uses is dated 20th January 1626-7 and is as follows :—

To all Christian people to whom this present writing shall come Henry Smith of London Esq. sendeth greeting in our Lord God everlasting.

Whereas the said Henry Smith by indenture bearing date the twentieth day of October 1620 in the seventeeth year of the reign of our late sovereign lord King James of famous memory made between him the said Henry Smith of the one part and the Right Honourable Robert Earl of Essex and Ewe the Right Honourable Richard Earl of Dorset Sir Edward Francis of Petworth in the county of Sussex Knight John Middleton of Horsham in the county of Sussex Esquire William Wingfield of London Esquire George Whitmore citizen and alderman of London and Richard Amhurst of Lewes in the said county of Sussex serjeant-at-law by the names in the said indenture expressed of the other part reciting that whereas the said Henry Smith by indenture made between him the said Henry Smith of the one part and the said Earl of Essex Earl of Dorset Sir Edward Francis John Middleton William Wingfield George Whitmore and Richard Amhurst of the other part and bearing date and being together delivered with the said recited indenture hath for the consideration therein expressed granted bargained sold and confirmed unto the said Earl of Essex Earl of Dorset Sir Edward Francis John Middleton William Wingfield George Whitmore and Richard Amhurst all those the manors and farms of Warbleton Southwecke and Iwood with their appurtenances in the county of Sussex and all that his messuage with the appurtenances in Silver-street London wherein he then dwelt and now dwelleth and all other his manors lands tenements and hereditaments leases for years extents rents charges and annuities due and payable or to be due and payable unto the said Henry Smith by reason of any estate in fee simple fee tayle for life lives or years or by any other ways or means whatsoever and all other the manors lands tenements and hereditaments of the said Henry Smith in the said county of Sussex city of London and in the county of Middlesex or elsewhere within the realm of England and all deeds charters and writings for touching and concerning the same to have hold and enjoy all and singular the said manors lands tenements hereditaments leases extents rents charges and annuities and all other the premises with all and singular their appurtenances whatsoever unto the said Earl of Essex Earl of Dorset Sir Edward Francis John Middleton William Wingfield George Whitmore and Richard Amhurst their heirs and assigns for ever to the only proper use and behoof of the said Earl of Esssex Earl of Dorset Sir Edward Francis John Middleton William Wingfield George Whitmore and Richard Amhurst their heirs and assigns for ever with a proviso or condition of revocation or making void the said recited grant bargain and sale and the estate therein limited by the said Henry Smith in his lifetime as in and by the said recited indenture whereunto relation being had more at large it doth and may appear and therein further reciting that whereas the said Henry Smith by one other indenture made between him of the one part and the said John Middleton William Wingfield George Whitmore and Richard Amhurst of the other part and bearing the date of the said former recited indenture did for the considerations therein expressed grant assign and set over unto the said John Middleton William Wingfield George Whitmore and Richard Amhurst all his ready money except one hundred pounds thereof and all his debts of what nature kind or condition soever and all his bonds bills statutes recognizances and assurances whatsoever for the same and all the yearly sum and sums of money due and payable or to be paid upon any mortgage or other condition or agreement and all his household stuff and implements of household whatsoever and all his goods and chattels real and personal of what kind quality or condition soever except also as in the said indenture is excepted as in and by the same indenture likewise more at large appeareth and it was in and by the same indenture published expressed and declared that it was the true intent and meaning of all the said parties to the same indentures that the said grant bargain and sale and the said assignment of the said ready money debts goods and chattels and all other goods in the said recited indenture mentioned and expressed was to these intents and purposes *viz.* that out of the yearly rents and profits of the said manors lands and premises should yearly be paid and answered to the said Henry Smith five hundred pounds per annum for and towards his maintenance and livelihood and all the residue of the rents issues and profits of the said manors farms lands and premises should be paid and employed to and for such uses intents and purposes and to such person and persons and for such time and times and in such manner and form as the said Henry Smith by any writing or writings to be by him sealed signed and delivered in the presence of two credible witnesses or more or by his last will and testament in writing to be by him signed sealed and allowed as his will in the presence of such witnesses as aforesaid should be limited assigned nominated and appointed and in default of such limitation assignment nomination or appointment or of such or so much as should not be by him so limited and appointed to such charitable use and uses for relief of poor prisoners hurt and maimed soldiers poor maids' marriages setting-up of poor apprentices amending of highways losses sustained by fire or shipwreck or otherwise as they the said Earl of Essex Earl of Dorset Sir Edward Francis John Middleton William Wingfield George Whitmore and Richard Amhurst their heirs or assigns should from time to time think most meet and convenient as in and by the said indentures relation being thereunto had more at large it doth and may appear.

And whereas also the said Henry Smith by his indenture bearing date the 12th day of June in the two-and-twentieth year of the reign of our said late sovereign lord King James of England &c. and of Scotland the seven-and-fiftieth made between him the said Henry Smith of the one part and the said Robert Earl of Essex Sir Edward Francis George Whitmore Richard Amhurst John Middleton and William Wingfield of the other part hath ratified allowed and confirmed the said grant bargain and sale of all and singular the manors lands and premises in the said first-recited indenture mentioned unto the said Earl of Essex Sir Edward Francis George Whitmore Richard Amhurst John Middleton and William Wingfield and hath thereby remised released and revoked the proviso or condition for power of revocation therein mentioned as in and by the same indenture thereunto relation being had more at large appeareth.

And whereas also the said Henry Smith by one other indenture bearing date the same twelfth day of June 1625 and made between the said Henry Smith of the one part and the said George Whitmore Richard Amhurst John Middleton and William Wingfield of the other part hath ratified allowed and confirmed the said grant and assignment of all and singular the premises in the same indenture mentioned unto the said George Whitmore Richard Amhurst John Middleton and William Wingfield and hath thereby also remised released and revoked the proviso or condition therein also mentioned as in and by the same indenture likewise appeareth

And whereas also in and by one other indenture bearing date the same twelfth day of June 1625 in the said two-and-twentieth year of his said late Majesty's reign of England &c. and of Scotland the seven-and-fiftieth made between him the said Henry Smith of the one part and the said Earl of Essex Christopher Nevill Sir Richard Lumley Sir George Crooke Sir Edward Francis George Whitmore Richard Amhurst John Middleton William Wingfield George Lowe William Blake William Rolfe and Richard Gurnet of the other part it was expressed and declared and the true intent and meaning of all the parties to the same was that out of the yearly rents and profits of the said manors lands and all other the premises there should be yearly paid and answered to the said Henry Smith five hundred pounds per annum for and towards his maintenance and livelihood And the said Henry Smith did by the same indenture grant ratify allow and confirm unto the said Earl of Essex Christopher Nevill Sir Richard Lumley Sir George Crooke Sir Edward Francis George Whitmore Richard Amhurst John Middleton William Wingfield George Lowe William Blake William Rolfe and Richard Gurnet the full nomination limitation assignment and appointment of all and singular the rents issues and profits of the manors lands and of all other the premises before mentioned to such uses intents and purposes as are before in the said recited indenture set forth as they should from time to time think meet and convenient And the said Henry Smith did thereby remise release revoke and make void all power of limitation assignment or appointment of the same or any part thereof to any use or uses before by the said recited indenture to him reserved either by his last will or otherwise as freely and absolutely as if no such power had been thereby reserved to him the said Henry Smith and did also thereby express publish and declare that the rents issues and profits of all the said manors lands and tenements and all the said goods chattels debts credits and other things should be bestowed and employed by the said Earl of Essex Christopher Nevill Sir Richard Lumley Sir George Crooke Sir Edward Francis George Whitmore Richard Amhurst John Middleton William Wingfield George Lowe William Blake William Rolfe and Richard Gurnet or any seven or more of them or by their heirs or assigns to such charitable use and uses for and towards the relief of poor prisoners hurt and maimed soldiers poor maids' marriages setting up of poor apprentices amending of highways losses sustained by fire or shipwreck or otherwise to and for such charitable uses as they the said Earl of Essex Sir Christopher Nevill Sir Richard Lumley Sir George Crooke Sir Edward Francis George Whitmore Richard Amhurst John Middleton William Wingfield George Lowe William Blake William Rolfe and Richard Gurnet or any seven or more of them their heirs and assigns should from time to time think most meet and convenient And to those purposes the said Henry Smith did by the said last recited indenture for the consideration therein specified grant bargain sell assign and set over unto the said Earl of Essex, Sir Christopher Nevill Sir Richard Lumley Sir George Crooke Sir Edward Francis George Whitmore Richard Amhurst John Middleton William Wingfield George Lowe William Blake William Rolfe and Richard Gurnet their heirs and assigns all his manors lands tenements and hereditaments and all his leases debts bonds statutes and chattels with the like power and authority unto them as in and by the same indenture is granted and allowed unto them or any of them except and always reserved as in and by the said former recited indenture is excepted for the maintenance and livelihood of the said Henry Smith during only the time of his natural life, as in and by the said last recited indenture whereunto relation being had likewise more at large it doth and may appear.

And whereas notwithstanding the said several conveyances releases and revocations were absolute yet in regard the said manors lands tenements and hereditaments and the said leases money debts bonds statutes goods and chattels of the said Henry Smith hereinbefore mentioned and recited were his free and voluntary gift and act without any valuable consideration from any of the said parties trusted and for that some of the said parties trusted who were indebted to the said Henry Smith at the time of the making of the said several conveyances did not endeavour the performance of the said trust reposed in them according to the true intent and meaning of the said Henry Smith Therefore the said Henry Smith for redress thereof did exhibit his bill in his Majesty's honourable Court of Chancery against them the said Earl of Essex Sir Christopher Nevill Richard Lumley Sir George Crooke Sir Edward Francis George Whitmore Richard Amhurst John Middleton William Wingfield George Lowe William Blake, William Rolfe and Richard Gurnet unto which bill each of them the said parties trusted did put in his answer and thereby did confess that the said several conveyances were made by the said Henry Smith freely and voluntarily without any valuable consideration and did severally and respectively submit themselves to the order and direction of the said most honourable Court concerning the premises whereupon the said cause coming on to be heard in open Court the twentieth day of June now last passed before the date hereof it was in the presence of Counsel learned on all parts and in the presence of some of the said parties adjudged ordered and decreed by and with the consent of them the said Richard Amhurst and John Middleton that they the said Richard Amhurst and John Middleton should by good and sufficient conveyance and assurance in the law convey and assure to the residue of the said parties trusted and their heirs executors and administrators all such estate right title and interest as the said Henry Smith had conveyed unto them by the said several conveyances hereinbefore mentioned and that the residue of the said parties trusted should during the natural life of the said Henry Smith dispose of the rents issues and profits of the said manors messuages lands tenements and hereditaments and the said leases monies goods chattels debts bonds statutes and other personal estate to such of the said charitable uses before herein mentioned or for the purchasing of parsonages and rectories impropriate for the maintenance of religious preaching ministers or such other charitable uses and to be employed in such manner as the said Henry Smith should think fit limit declare and appoint as in and by the said bill answers and decree relation being thereto had more at large it doth and may appear.

Now therefore further know ye that for the better performance of the said charitable uses and settling thereof in such sort as that the same may have continuance for ever according to the true intent and meaning of the said Henry Smith the said Henry Smith doth hereby limit appoint and declare his true intent and meaning to be and doth hereby intreat them the said Earl of Essex Sir Christopher Nevill Sir Richard Lumley Sir George Crooke George Whitmore George Lowe William Blake William Rolfe Richard Gurnet and Henry Jackson of London Cheesemonger to see the same performed accordingly which he hopes they will vouchsafe to do the same tending to the advancement of religion piety and charity that is to say that they the said Earl of Essex Sir Christopher Nevill Sir Richard Lumley Sir George Crooke George Whitmore George Lowe William Blake William Rolfe Richard Gurnet and Henry Jackson and the heirs of the survivor of them shall employ and bestow such monies as they shall receive of the rents and revenues of the said manors lands tenements and hereditaments and of the monies debts or other personal estate of the said Henry Smith before mentioned for the purchasing of manors lands tenements and hereditaments to themselves or so many of them as shall be then living and their heirs but with this that the true intent and meaning of the said Henry Smith is and is hereby declared to be that they the said Earl of Essex Sir Christopher Nevill Sir Richard Lumley Sir George Crooke George Whitmore George Lowe William Blake William Rolfe Richard Gurnet and Henry Jackson or the survivors of them or the heirs of the survivor of them shall with all convenient speed procure from his Majesty his heirs or successors a licence under the great seal of England to be granted to the Governors of Christ's Hospital in London and their successors to receive and take the same in mortmain and that so soon as the said licence shall be so procured they the said Earl of Essex Sir Christopher Nevill Sir Richard Lumley Sir George Crooke George Whitmore George Lowe William Blake William Rolfe Richard Gurnet and Henry Jackson and the survivors of them and the heirs of the survivor of them shall by good and sufficient conveyance and assurance in the law convey and assure as well the said manors messuages lands tenements and hereditaments herein before mentioned as the said manors messuages lands tenements and other hereditaments to be purchased as aforesaid to the Governors of the said Hospital and their successors discharged of all incumbrances done by them and every of them to be by them employed according to the true intent and meaning of the said decree and of these presents and for and concerning such and so much of the said manors messuages lands tenements and hereditaments whereof the profits shall not be disposed of by the said Henry Smith during his life the same shall be employed and disposed by the said Earl of Essex Sir Christopher Nevill Sir Richard Lumley Sir George Crooke George Whitmore George Lowe William Blake William Rolfe Richard Gurnet and Henry Jackson according to the true intent and meaning of the said recited conveyances and decree In which said purchase and purchases so to be made of manors lands tenements and hereditaments as aforesaid the said Henry Smith doth desire that they the said Earl of Essex Sir Christopher Nevill Sir Richard Lumley Sir George Crooke George Whitmore George Lowe William Blake William Rolfe Richard Gurnet and Henry Jackson and the survivors of them and the heirs of the survivor of them shall so near as may conveniently be observe the proportion to purchase for every thousand pounds that they shall disburse and lay forth manors lands tenements or other hereditaments in fee simple of the clear yearly value of one hundred marks above all charges and reprises the charges of the making drawing and passing of the said assurances and of the procuring of the said licence to purchase in mortmain and all other charges for or by reason thereof or concerning the same or any of them or concerning any other thing in or touching the premises to be paid and borne out of the rents issues and profits of the said manors messuages lands tenements and hereditaments so to be conveyed as aforesaid.

Item for the avoiding of corruption in the collection receiving distribution and payment of the several sums of money heretofore given limited appointed or assigned and hereafter to be given limited appointed or assigned by the said Henry Smith during his life-time or to be purchased or conveyed by the said Earl of Essex Sir Christopher Nevill Sir Richard Lumley Sir George Crooke George Whitmore George Low William Blake William Rolfe Richard Gurnet and Henry Jackson or the survivor or survivors of them or the heirs of the survivor of them after his decease and to be yearly paid out of the rents issues or profits of the said manors messuages lands tenements and hereditaments hereafter to be purchased according to the true intent and meaning of these presents for the yearly relief of the poor of any parish or for the marriage of poor maids or putting forth of poor children to be apprentices shall yearly be received as the said rents shall grow due and payable by the churchwardens and overseers of the poor of each of the said parishes respectively that is to say the churchwardens and overseers of the poor of each of the said parishes respectively to receive the rent of so much land as is or shall be given limited assigned or appointed to be employed as aforesaid within that parish wherein they shall be churchwardens and overseers as aforesaid.

Item the said Henry Smith for the better security of the performance of the said charitable gift doth hereby limit and appoint and declare his intent and meaning to be that the churchwardens and overseers of the poor of each of the said parishes for relief of whose poor such gift assignment limitation or appointment shall be made as aforesaid immediately they shall enter into the said offices and before they shall meddle with the receipt of the said rent or any part thereof shall become bound by obligation in double the value of such yearly receipt to the parson or vicar of the said parish to collect and receive the said rent and to employ and bestow the same according to the true intent and meaning of these presents; which said parson or vicar to whom such security shall be so given shall before the said churchwardens or overseers of the poor of the said parish shall intermeddle with the receipt of the said rents or any of them certify the said obligation uncancelled to the Governors of the said Hospital for the time being and in default of such security to be so given or certificate made of the said obligation that parish wherein such default shall be made to lose the benefit of the said gift limitation or assignment so made or to be made for that year wherein such default shall be made as aforesaid.

Item for the better direction of the churchwardens and overseers of the said several parishes in the distribution of such sums of money as are or shall be given assigned or appointed to the said charitable uses before mentioned the said Henry Smith doth hereby limit and declare and doth think fit and appoint that the said churchwardens and overseers of the poor of the said several parishes respectively shall give and distribute the said monies given limited assigned or appointed to the said charitable uses to and for the relief of aged poor or infirm people married persons having more children born in lawful wedlock than their labours can maintain poor orphans such poor people as keep themselves and families to labour and put forth their children to be apprentices at the ages of fifteen years wherein each of the said churchwardens and overseers of each of the said parishes are to observe such course in disposing of the said rents as that a stock may be provided and always in readiness to set such of the said persons to work as are able to labour and take pains and not to or for the relief of any persons who are given to excessive drinking whoremongers common swearers pilferers or otherwise notoriously scandalous or to any persons that have been incorrigible or disobedient to those whose servants they have been or to any vagrant persons or such as have no constant dwelling or receive any inmate or inmates to dwell in house with them or have not inhabited in that parish by the space of five years next before such distribution to be made or being able refuse to work labour and take pains.

Item the said Henry Smith to the intent and purpose aforesaid doth further limit assign and appoint and declare his intent and meaning to be that for the better ordering and government of the poor of the said several parishes and disposing of the sums of money given to the uses aforesaid the churchwardens of each of the said parishes shall during the time they shall continue in the said offices and places once in every month at the least upon the Sabbath day after evening prayer meet in the church of the said parish to consider of the estate of the poor of the said parish which of them have most need of relief and shall also between the feasts of Easter and Whitsuntide next after the end of every year wherein the said churchwardens and overseers of the poor of that parish or any of them shall have continued in either of the said offices or places openly and publicly in the church of the said parish after evening prayer upon some sabbath day upon notice and warning thereof given openly in that parish church immediately after the end of morning prayer make a true and perfect account in a book to be fairly written and kept for that purpose of all their receipts and disbursements for and during the year then next before of all such sums of money as they or any of them shall receive of the said monies given to the uses aforesaid which said account shall be openly read and published in the church of the said parish on the Sabbath day next after the taking of the said account immediately after the end of morning prayer there and a copy thereof fairly written and transcribed under the hands of the said churchwardens and overseers that did make the same account shall cause to be affixed in a table to the wall of the said church in some convenient place there to remain by the space of fourteen days to the intent the same may be publicly seen read and perused and exceptions taken thereunto if there be just cause and the same exceptions reformed and amended and further that the said churchwardens and overseers of the poor that shall have so passed the said account shall within ten days then next following after the end of the said fourteen days send or deliver or cause to be sent or delivered under the hands of the parson or vicar of the said parish and of the said churchwardens and overseers as shall pass the said account and such others as shall be present thereat a copy of said account to the governors of the said hospital for the time being and that if the said churchwardens and overseers of the poor of any of the said parishes shall fail in performance of any of the premises that then as a penalty mulct or punishment for such neglect the poor of that parish shall not have of the gift of the said Henry Smith for one year then next ensuing after such neglect but the benefit thereof to go for that time to the poor of the said hospital.

Item the said Henry Smith doth further by these presents limit and appoint and declare his intent and meaning to be that the said sums of money given limited assigned or appointed to or for the relief of the impotent and aged poor of the said parishes respectively shall be distributed bestowed and employed in apparel of one colour with some badge or other mark that the same may be known to be the gift of the said Henry Smith or else in bread and flesh or fish upon each Sabbath-day publicly in the parish churches of each of the said parishes.

Item the said Henry Smith doth further by these presents declare his intent and meaning to be that although the estate and interest as well of all the said manors messuages lands tenements and hereditaments by the said Henry Smith conveyed as aforesaid as those that are hereafter to be purchased are hereby directed to be settled in the governors of the said hospital and their successors yet such leases copyhold and customary estates as are to be made thereof shall be bargained and contracted for by the churchwardens and overseers of the poor of such parish for the relief of the poor whereof the profits of the said lands so to be leased or disposed are or shall be according to the true intent and meaning of these presents assigned limited or appointed to be employed to the intent the best yearly value may be made thereof and that the said governors of the said hospital and their successors shall make such leases and estates and to such persons as the said churchwardens and overseers shall appoint in writing under their hands and seals reserving such rent and with such covenants conditions and agreements as they shall agree upon so as such leases or estates exceed not the term of one-and-twenty years or three lives in possession and so as the lands so to be letten be in the best manner that may be letten at the best improved yearly rents and not for great fines and small rents except for copyhold lands only which may be granted upon fines.

In witness whereof the said Henry Smith hath hereunto set his hand and seal the six-and-twentieth day of January in the second year of the reign of our Sovereign Lord Charles by the grace of God King of England Scotland France and Ireland Defender of the Faith &c. 1626.

MR. HENRY SMITH made his Will dated 24th April, 1627, of which the following is a Copy viz:—

IN the name of GOD Amen The four-and twentieth day of April in the third year of the reign of our Sovereign Lord Charles by the grace of God King of England Scotland France and Ireland Defender of the Faith, &c. I Henry Smith of Silver Street in London Esq. being in health of body and of good and perfect memory and understanding (praises be therefore given unto God) do make and ordain this my last will and testament in writing in manner and form following that is to say first and principally I commend my soul into the hands of Almighty God my heavenly Father trusting assuredly by the only death and passion of JESUS CHRIST his son my only Saviour and Redeemer to have remission of all my sins and to be made an inheritor of eternal life And I commend my body to the earth whereof it is made to be buried in such place and in such decent manner as to my executors hereafter named shall be thought fit there to remain in Christian burial until the resurrection of all flesh which I assuredly believe and expect And as touching the disposing of my lands and goods wherewith it hath pleased GOD to bless me first I give and bequeath unto Henry Henn Gent. sometimes my servant the sum of one hundred pounds to be paid unto him within one year after my decease for which one hundred pounds I have given him my bond already. *Item* I give and bequeath for the use of the poor captives being slaves under the Turkish pirates the sum of one thousand pounds which sum of one thousand pounds my will and meaning is shall be laid forth and bestowed in the purchase of lands of inheritance to the value of threescore pounds per annum at the least the rents and profits whereof shall be yearly paid and distributed unto such person and persons as from time to time shall be appointed and intrusted for the collection of the charity of well-disposed persons with the intent that the same my gift shall continue in perpetuity and shall be so paid and delivered at the discretion of my said executors and their heirs, and of the survivors of them and of the Lord Mayor and Sheriffs of the City of London for the time being for and towards the relief and ransom of the said poor captives and slaves *Item* I give and devise for the use and relief of the poorest of my kindred such as are not able to work for their living *viz.* sick aged and impotent persons and such as cannot maintain their own charge the sum of one thousand pounds which said one thousand pounds my will and meaning is shall be laid forth and bestowed in the purchase of lands of inheritance of the value of threescore pounds per annum at the least and the rents and profits thereof to be paid yearly unto them and to be distributed amongst them by my said executors and their heirs and by the said Lord Mayor of London and the Sheriffs for the time being as most need shall be from time to time And my will and meaning is that in the bestowing and distributing of my estate and goods to the poor to charitable uses which is according to my intent and desire those of my kindred which are poor aged impotent or any other way unable to help themseves should be chiefly preferred and respected. *Item* I give and devise unto the children of one ——— Daborne late of Richmond carpenter deceased to be divided amongst them part and part alike the sum of fifty pounds to be paid within three months next after my decease *Item* I give and devise unto Richard Owen gentleman servant to the Dean of Westminster the sum of one hundred pounds to be paid unto him within one year next after my decease *Item* I give and bequeath unto and for the use of the poor of the town of Wandsworth the sum of five hundred pounds which said five hundred pounds my will and meaning is shall be paid unto some sufficient inhabitants of the said town of Wandsworth in trust to buy lands of inheritance the rents and profits whereof to be yearly paid to and for the relief of the said poor there for ever for the true performance whereof according to the purport of such articles as are already agreed on by the bailiffs and burgesses of the town of Kingston in that behalf my will and desire is that my said executors upon payment of the said money shall take some such sufficient covenants and assurances from the said inhabitants of the said town of Wandsworth as shall be by my said executors thought meet *Item* in the same manner to be bestowed and secured I give and devise unto and for the poor of the town of Reigate the sum of one thousand pounds *Item* I give unto the child of my servant Michael Montgomery the sum of ten pounds and to my servants Michael and Mary Vavasour to each of them per annum ten pounds during their lives *Item* I do clearly release and forgive unto John Walker of Billingsgate the sum of two hundred pounds which he oweth unto me upon several bonds for money lent him *Item* I give unto the Right Honourable Mary countess of Dorset the sum of two hundred pounds to be paid unto her within a year after my decease to be disposed by her to and amongst her children equally or otherwise as to her honour shall be thought best *Item* I give will and devise the several debts and sums of money due and owing unto me by Sir Edward Francis Sir Richard Lumley and John Middleton amounting to ten thousand pounds in the whole or thereabouts to and for the purchasing and buying in of appropriations for the relief and maintenance of godly preachers and the better furtherance of knowledge and religion to be bestowed at and by the discretion of my executors accordingly *Item* my will and meaning is that all or the most part of the legacies and sums of money which by this my last will or otherwise I have given or intended to the use or relief of the poor of any parish town or place shall be so ordered continued or managed yearly and from time to time for the setting of the poor on work and for binding them apprentices and for the teaching and education of poor children as is now used or begun within the town of Dorchester in the county of Dorset and according to my deed of uses last made *Item* I give and devise the sum of one hundred and fifty pounds for the buying of a fellowship in Cambridge in some college there to continue for eight years and so long to be enjoyed by Mr. Costender's son and at the end of those eight years to be surrendered by him unto and to the use of my nephew Henry Jackson son of Henry Jackson the elder one of my executors hereafter named to continue to him during his life and after to such of my kindred as shall be capable of the place or fellowship from time to time and my will and meaning is that my executors hereafter named shall at their discretion lend the sum of one hundred pounds to some such person as shall need *gratis* for one half year by twenty pounds in a parcel and when the same is repaid to lend it out to others for other six months and so to continue from time to time my executors taking good security for the repayment thereof *Item* I give unto my executors hereafter named and to my feoffees which I have trusted for the behoof of the poor to each of them the sum of five pounds to buy them rings *Item* I give unto one Mrs. Price now or sometimes a teacher of children my kinswoman, the sum of ten pounds to be paid within one year after my decease *Item* I give to Rebecca Collins daughter of George Collins, the sum of ten pounds *Item* I give unto Mr. ——Hughs the sum of ten pounds *Item* I give to the two daughters of Sir William Bond Winifred and Elizabeth the sum of fifteen pounds whereof one pound is a debt due to me by their brother John Bond *Item* I give to the poor of the parish where I dwell five pounds *Item* I give to the poor of St. Anne's parish the like sum of five pounds *Item* I give to the poor of St. Dunstan's in the East the sum of five pounds *Item* I give to Mr. S. Butcher the sum of ten pounds *Item* I give to Ferdinand Clerke the sum of twenty shillings *Item* I give to Sir Robert Philips and his lady and children one hundred pounds *Item* I give to the eldest lady Delaware, wife of Thomas late Lord Delaware the sum of one hundred pounds

Item I give to Mr. William Rowley the sum of twenty pounds *Item* I give to John Franklyn and one Weaver and Jane Llyd my neighbours to each of them twenty shillings *Item* I give to Mr. Doctor Lloyd a mourning gown and ten pounds in money *Item* I give to my nephew Henry Jackson one of my executors and to the said John Walker the sum of one hundred pounds to be disposed by them to such poor as they shall think fit *Item* I give and devise unto Godfrey Mazlchill the sum of five pounds *Item* I give and devise to Henry Smith of the Old Change five pounds and to good wife Seabright twenty shillings and to Mr. Paytie ten shillings *Item* I do hereby will and devise unto the poor of the town of Richmond the sum of one thousand pounds due and owing unto me by Mr. Serjeant Amhurst to be laid forth and bestowed by my executors for the purchase of lands of inheritance to and for the use of the poor of the said town in perpetuity to continue unto them under the same trust as my other gifts to other towns do and my will and meaning is that Mr. Henry Henn shall be one of my feoffees in the place of Sir Edward Francis *Item* I give to Augustine Daborne the gardener ten pounds And whereas by an indenture bearing date the twentieth day of October in the seventeenth year of our late Sovereign Lord King James over this realm of England &c. I did grant bargain sell and confirm unto the Right Honourable Richard then Earl of Dorset since deceased Robert now Earl of Essex Sir Edward Francis Knight John Middleton William Wingfield George Whitmore and Richard Amhurst then Esq. now Serjeant at the law and to their heirs in trust and with power of revocation all those the manors and farms of Warbleton Southwood and Iwood with the appurtenances in the county of Sussex and my messuage in Silver-street wherein I now dwell and all other my manors lands tenements hereditaments leases for years extents rents charges and annuities to me due or to be due and payable by reason of any estate in fee simple fee tayle for life lives or years or by any other ways or means whatsoever And also all other my manors lands tenements and hereditaments in the said county of Sussex city of London and county of Middlesex or elsewhere within the realm of England And whereas also I did by another indenture of the same date grant assign and set over unto the said John Middleton William Wingfield George Whitmore and Richard Amhurst with like power of revocation all my ready money (except one hundred pounds) and all my debts bonds bills statutes recognizances and assurances for the same and all yearly sum and sums of money due and payable upon any mortgage condition or agreement and all my household stuff goods and chattels real and personal whatsoever (except as in the said indenture is excepted) which lands and premises were so conveyed in trust to uses and with power left in me of revocation or alteration at my pleasure as by another indenture bearing date the said twentieth day of October appeareth And whereas sithence by some indirect and colourable pretences by some other deed since made it is pretended that I have released and discharged the said power of revocation or alteration of uses left and reserved which releases (if any such be) were and yet are contrary to my true intent and meaning And whereas the said Sir Edward Francis John Middleton and Richard Amhurst and one Sir Richard Lumley Knight stand severally indebted and did stand severally indebted unto me in divers great sums of money upon several assurances which debts and sums of money my will and meaning neither is nor ever was to release unto them or any of them and therefore I do hereby give and devise unto my executors hereafter named and to their heirs and assigns upon trust and to the uses hereinbefore expressed all such debts sum and sums of money as are or were owing or ought to be due or payable unto me by the said Sir Edward Francis Sir Richard Lumley John Middleton and Richard Amhurst or any of them to the uses aforesaid and all manors messuages lands and tenements whatsoever to me granted mortgaged or assured of or for the same and my will and meaning is and I do hereby expressly declare and appoint my said executors hereafter named to have and take demand and require of and from the said Earl of Essex Sir Edward Francis John Middleton William Wingfield and Richard Amhurst and of and from all other person or persons which by virtue or colour of any trust or grant by me made to or had and reposed in them or any of them or otherwise shall have or receive any sum or sums of money rents or other profits whatsoever which did or should belong unto me from time to time just and true accompts thereof and to their utmost power shall see the same to be justly and truly bestowed and given according to the true meaning of this my last will and testament And I do hereby give grant and devise unto my said executors hereafter named and to their heirs and assigns not only all my manors messuages lands tenements and herditaments whatsoever with their appurtenances situate and being in the city of London and in the counties of Middlesex Kent Sussex Gloucester and Worcester or in any of them or elsewhere within the realm of England but also all and singular my goods chattels plate household stuff debts sum and sums of money jewels and all other my real and personal estate whatsoever (my debts and funeral expenses first discharged) upon trust and confidence and to the uses intents and purposes expressed and declared herein and by my last deed and writing by me sealed for declaration of my uses and now enrolled lately in his Majesty's High Court of Chancery and which from time to time shall be limited and declared by me by writing under my hand and seal sufficiently testifieth and for want of such limitation declaration or appointment then to be paid and bestowed in charitable uses to the relief and maintenance of poor towns in the same manner as I have herein formerly appointed to the towns of Wandsworth and Kingston at the discretion of my executors and my will and meaning is that all such sum and sums of money as by the true meaning of this my last will should be bestowed in charitable uses or should come to the hands of the poor therein mentioned shall within six years next after my decease or sooner if the same may be conveniently gotten in be paid and distributed amongst them accordingly And my will is that all my said executors and the survivors of them from time to time shall join jointly in the trust hereby reposed in them and shall yearly make a just and true account of all their proceedings therein unto my overseers hereafter named who shall in all differences and doubts arising amongst my said executors compose the same according to their best discretions And I do hereby as much as in me is revoke repeal and disannul all former wills and testaments by me made and all former trusts grants assurances conveyances authorities and powers whatsoever by me made or granted to any person or persons whatsoever touching or concerning my said lands or goods or any of them which have been by me questioned or complained of in his Majesty's High Court of Chancery And I do hereby make nominate and appoint George Whitmore alderman of London George Lowe William Blake William Rolfe Esq. Richard Garnard cloth-worker and Henry Jackson grocer of London to be the executors of this my last will and testament earnestly praying them to be careful in seeing this my last will and testament duly performed And I do hereby nominate Mr. Justice Crook Sir Christopher Nevill Mr. Alderman Parkhurst and George Duncomb Esq. to be the overseers of this my last will and testament In witness whereof I the said Henry Smith to this my present last will and testament containing seven sheets of paper have severally subscribed my name and have set to my seal at the top thereof the day and year first above written Henry Smith subscribed as aforesaid with the proper hand of the said Henry Smith in the presence of Thomas Canon Ja. Aston William Rowley Thomas Carter sealed published and declared by the said Henry Smith (who was of perfect memory) to be his last will and testament in the presence of us witnesses whose names are hereunder written Thomas Canon Thomas Costerdine Edw. Brightwen Francis Billing John Honeybourne.

Memorandum that Henry Smith late of St. Olave's in Silver-street London after the making and declaring of his last will and testament in writing did on or about the twenty-eighth of September one thousand six hundred and twenty-seven by word of mouth give and bequeath unto his nephew Henry Jackson the sum of one thousand pounds and to his servants Michael Montgomery and Mary Vavasour ten pounds a-piece but willed that the said ten pounds bequeathed to the said Michael should not come to his hands but should be preserved and kept for his the said Michael's child being present George Lowe Henry Jackson Michael Montgomery and Mary Vavasour *Item* he did at another time give and bequeath to Sir Thomas Canon Knight to buy him a ring one pound *Item* to Thomas Noakes ten pounds *Item* to Jane Mayson of Bolton one pound *Item* he bequeathed to John Tench his chirurgeon ten pounds and a mourning gown Moreover the said testator being asked which of his kindred he meant and intended in and by those words the poorest of his kindred &c. in the legacy of a thousand pounds bequeathed in his will to be laid out and bestowed in the purchase of lands of inheritance of the value of sixty pounds per annum and the rents and profits to be yearly unto them &c. made answer that his meaning was thereby the poorest of his sisters' children and their children successively or like in effect.

Probatum &c. Vicessimo tertio Januarii Anno Domini in &c. 1627 Juramentis Domini Willielm. Militis Georgii Lowe Richardi Garnard et Henrici Jackson Executorum &c. Reserata &c.

Probatum &c. decimo nono Junii Anno Domini 1628 Juramento Willielmi Rolfe Armigeri Executoris etiam &c. Reserata &c. Georgii Whitmore &c.

Barrington 2.

The Stoughton Estate, from which St. Botolph Without Aldersgate, with other parishes, derive their benefit, was purchased by the Trustees. It consists of a house and 315 a. 3 r. 9 p. of land, situate in the parishes of Stoughton, Houghton, Errington, and Busby, in Leicestershire. It was last let to Major Powys Kech, in April 1844, at a rent of £630, whose lease expired at Michaelmas 1865. On the expiration of the lease the Lessee declined to take a renewal, but offered to make an Exchange, and the following letter was sent to each of the parishes interested:—

GENTLEMEN,

The Lease of the Farm will expire at Michaelmas 1865, Major Powys Kech, the Lessee, says that he shall not take another lease, but he has offered to give in exchange some freehold tithe rents producing a clear income of about £650, and £3,500 in money. The farm was let by Auction, in April 1844, for £630, which was more than Mr. Clutton then thought it worth.

The allowance for materials, for repairs, and draining, has reduced the rent on an average to £616 : 5s.

The quantity of land is 315 a. 2 r. 39 p. It is underlet to a farmer at £580, and would have no value for building; but being the only farm in the Parish, not belonging to Major Kech, and little more than a mile from his house, it is an object to him to obtain it.

The following is Mr. Clutton's Report on the proposal :—

"The Stoughton Estate is let at £630, assuming that the lessee is "bound to do all repairs and insure, and that the farm would again "let for the same rent. Thirty years' purchase would be a moderate "number of years to capitalize the income, viz.—

$$\begin{array}{r} £630 \\ 30 \\ \hline £18,900 \end{array}$$

"Weston Tithe Rent Charge.......................... 762 7 2
"Outgoings :—
    "Land Tax................................. 17 5 5
    "Rates...................................... 52 10 0
    "Collection and Chancel 43 0 0
                                             ——— 112 15 5
                                                 ——————
                                                 649 11 9

"Say net value.. 650 0 0
"Years purchase.. 24 0 0
                                                         ——————
                                                         15,600 0 0
"Delapidations of the Chancel..................... 300 0 0
                                                         ——————
                                                         15,300 0 0
"Sum offered for equality of Exchange 3,500 0 0
                                                         ——————
                                                         £18,800 0 0

"Scarcely any rent charges sell for so much as 24 years purchase "but this appears to be easy of collection."

The above Report was made by Mr. Clutton without adverting to the deduction from the rent of the farm for repairs and insurance.

If a majority in interest of the Parishes, entitled to the rent, approve of the exchange, the Trustees will entertain and consider Major Kech's proposal.

The following are the Parishes entitled:—

Andover	Ramsey	St. Botolph's
Broadhinton	Reigate	St Sepulchre
Bedworth	St. John Bedwardine	Thetford
Bledlow	Shapwick	Waterbeach
Dovercourt	St. John's Chester	Wandsworth
East Grinstead	St. Michael's ditto	Warminster
East Dereham	St. Giles' Cripplegate	Westbury

You are requested to inform us, whether it is the wish of your Parish that an exchange should take place on the above mentioned terms if a larger sum than £3,500 for equality of exchange should not be offered by Major Kech, or on the terms of his paying £1000 more, or any greater sum.

We are, Gentlemen,
Your obedient servants,
BRAY & Co.

4th January 1862.

The Churchwardens and Overseers of this Parish, having considered the matter fully, declined to entertain the application for an Exchange. And it is presumed that the other Parishes did the same, as it was shortly after determined to let the same by public Auction, in the manner directed by an Order in Chancery, of which the following is a copy:—

BY an Order of the High Court of Chancery, made the 29th day of October 1774, in a Cause between His Majesty's Attorney-General and the *Earl of Ashburnham* and others, the Trustees of the Estates settled by *Henry Smith*, Esq., and by his Trustees to charitable uses, IT WAS ORDERED, That the Trustees of the said Charity Estates for the Time being should, at least eighteen calendar Months before the Expiration of the then present and all future Lease or Leases to be granted of the said Estates, or any Part thereof, send Circular Letters to the Churchwardens or Overseers, for the Time being, of the several and respective Towns and Parishes interested in the said Charity, giving them Notice of the Time of the Expiration of such Lease and Leases, and also giving them at least three Months' Notice of the Time and Place of letting the said Estates upon any new Lease or Leases; and that the said Trustees should advertise in the Leicester and Northampton Journals or Newspapers, and also in one or two of the London Evening Papers, once a Week, for at least three Months before the Time of such letting, that the said Estates would be let to the best Bidder, at a public Auction to be held at Leicester, at a Time and Place to be expressed in such Advertisement; and that the Churchwardens and Overseers, for the Time being, of the several Towns and Parishes interested in the said Charity, or the major Part of them, should be at Liberty, by Writing under their Hands, to appoint an Agent to attend at such Time and Place, to set and let the said Charity Estates to the best Bidder, upon Condition that such Bidder should be afterwards approved of by the said Trustees, and which Condition, at the Time of letting, was to be considered as Part of the Terms upon which the Biddings were to be taken; and that the said Trustees should be also at Liberty (if they thought proper) to appoint an Agent to be present at such letting; but in case no Agent should be appointed by the said Churchwardens and Overseers of the said Towns and Parishes, or the major Part of them, or, if appointed, such Agent should not attend at the Time and Place appointed for such letting, that then the Agent for the said Trustees should be at Liberty to let the said Estates to the best Bidder upon the Condition therein before-mentioned : that the said Trustees should grant Leases of the said Charity Estates for any Term of Years not exceeding twenty-one Years in possession, upon the best and most improved Rent, without taking any Fine or Premium for the same, under and subject to all such Covenants as were usually contained in Leases of Lands granted in that Part of the Country where the said Charity Estates lay: that the Churchwardens and Overseers, for the Time being, of any of the said several Towns and Parishes should be at Liberty to have attested Copies of any Lease or Leases then subsisting, or thereafter to be granted, of any Part of the said Charity Estate, upon applying to and paying the Treasurer or Treasurers of the said Charity a reasonable Fee for the same.

The following Report was then received, shewing the particulars of the Estate proposed to be given in Exchange, viz.:—

57, Great Russell Street, W.C.
15th *June* 1865.

Gentlemen,
We now send you the particulars of the Exchange which Mr. Keck has offered to make.

The Estate to be given in exchange by Mr. Keck consists of a Farm in the Parish of Thurlaston, Leicestershire, called Manor House Farm, containing 238 a. 3 r. 35 p., and another farm called Hoc Field Farm in the same Parish, containing 241 a. 1 r. 33 p. The Stoughton Estate, as we have informed you, consists of 315 a. 2 r. 39 p., and is let for £630, but it is underlet to the occupying Tenant at about £530.

The following is Mr. Clutton's Report:—

"We have viewed the land at Thurlaston, Leicestershire, proposed to be given to the Trustees in exchange for the Great Stoughton Farm, as set out in the enclosed particulars.

"The property is compact, and the land is of very good quality. The buildings, although much better than those at Great Stoughton, are, some of them, old. Some new buildings have been erected within two or three years, and are very substantial. To complete the farm buildings will require an outlay of about £1200. The money, to carry out this, could be borrowed from the Government or one of the Land Improvement Companies for a term, repayable by Instalments.

"If the Great Stoughton Farm is retained, a much larger outlay should be made upon the buildings, which are worn out with age, to enable a Tenant to do justice to the Land.

"The Thurlaston Farms are at present let at fair rents to substantial Tenants, who manage the land extremely well, and we should advise the Trustees to continue them as Tenants in the event of their acquiring the Estate, first putting the Buildings in order and binding the Tenants to repair. The Trustees would then have a well secured rental (taking off £100 to pay interest and repay loan which would be more than sufficient) of £799 as against the present income of £630 derived from Great Stoughton, which is not well secured, the present occupying Tenant paying only a net rental of £518 : 7s. per annum.

"We estimate the value in fee of the Thurlaston property at £25,800.

"We should strongly advise the Trustees to carry out the Exchange as it appears to us so greatly to their advantage.

"Mr. Keck is willing to pay all expenses attending the transaction.

"We shall be obliged by your informing us whether you approve of leaving it to the Trustees to complete the Exchange if on further investigation they are satisfied that it will be advantageous to the Charity, and having the approval of the Charity Commissioners."

We remain, Gentlemen,
Your obedient servants,
BRAY & Co.

The Trustees of the Charity in the meantime would appear to have laid the matter before the Charity Commissioners, as the Churchwardens, on the 2nd of March 1866, received the following communication :—

CHARITY COMMISSION.

8, YORK STREET, ST. JAMES'S SQUARE, S. W.
2nd March, 1866.

HENRY SMITH'S CHARITY,
THE STOUGHTON ESTATE.

GENTLEMEN,

The Trustees of the above mentioned Charity have made an application to the Charity Commissioners for authority to exchange this Estate for an Estate belonging to Mr. Keck, in the parish of Thurlaston, in the County of Leicester, containing 480 a. 1 r. 28 p.

It has been represented that the particulars of the contemplated exchange have been already forwarded to you.

I have to inform you that, under the circumstances, the transaction is apparently so beneficial to the Charity, that the Commissioners will be prepared to give effect to the proposed exchange.

I am, Gentlemen,
Your obedient servant,
HENRY W. VANE,
Secretary.

The Churchwardens of St. Botolph,
Aldersgate Street, E.C.

This Exchange has not yet been carried out, but is still in negociation.

There is no information as to the amount of personal Estate which came to the hands of the Trustees, but they are now in the possession of several Estates, some of which appears to have been purchased by the Donor in his life-time, and others to have been conveyed to the Trustees after his death.

Nothwithstanding the directions given by Mr. Henry Smith, it does not appear that the Governors of Christ's Hospital had ever any concern in the management of this Charity. Trustees have been regularly appointed from time to time with the approval of the Archbishop of Canterbury, and the Lord Chancellor, according to the directions contained in the Decree of the Court of Chancery before mentioned.

The Original Allotments to the different parishes appear to have been made in 1641, as under:

20th December 1641. By Deed Inrolled in Chancery 1st April, 18 Charles I., the Earl of Essex, Viscount Lumley, Sir Richard Gurney, Sir Christopher Neville, Sir George Whitmore, William Rolfe, Henry Henne, and Henry Jackson, the then surviving Trustees divided the Rents in the following manner, viz.:—

	£	s.	d.		£	s.	d.
Andover	10	0	0	Shapwick	5	0	0
Broadhinton	7	0	0	St. John Chesier			
Bedworth	8	0	0	St. Michael Chester	11	0	0
Bledlow	5	0	0	St. Giles Cripplegate	20	0	0
Dover Court	6	13	4	St. Botolph Aldersgate	20	0	0
East Grinstead	15	0	0	St. Sepulchre	20	0	0
East Dearham	4	0	0	Thetford	10	0	0
Ramsey	6	13	4	Waterbeach	6	13	4
Ryegate	20	0	0	Wansworth	20	0	0
St. John Bedwardine	7	0	0	Warminster	10	0	0
				Wesbury	8	0	0

The Charity varies in amount; the parish of St. Botolph Aldersgate, in 1768, only received £13 : 12s.; in 1793 it received £27 : 9s.; in 1817 £47 : 6s. 7d., and in 1865 it received £54 : 13s.

It may not be uninteresting to know that this Benefactor to the parish was born at Wandsworth, Surrey, in 1548. On the 9th of February 1608, he was elected Alderman for the Ward of Farringdon Without, and in the Corporation Books is described as Citizen and Salter. He died 30th January 1627, aged 79 years, and was buried in the Church at Wandsworth.

OBSERVATIONS.

It will be seen by the above that the value of the Gift on the first allotment in 1641 was £20, while in 1865 it was £54 : 13s.

This Gift is distributed annually in Bread, Tea, Coffee, and Sugar, to poor persons who have resided in the parish for five years and upwards.

MR. HENRY FRYER'S GIFT.

Henry Fryer was seized in fee of the Manor of Harleton in the County of Cambridge, and of a messuage wherein the said Henry Fryer dwelt in the parish of St. Buttolph Without Aldersgate, and of ten messuages built with brick in Pilkington Place, and of five messuages built with timber in Pilkington Place, and of nineteen other messuages in Pilkington Place and Little Brittain, and of three messuages in Aldersgate Street, in the tenures of Christian Netleton, John Wright, and Giles Townsend, and of one messuage in the parish of St. Giles Without Cripplegate, then late in the tenure of Thomas Bennett, Esq.

12th April, 2 Car.

The said Henry Fryer, by indenture and recoveries, settled the said manor, messuages, and premises upon himself for life; and afterwards to the use of such person and persons and for such estate and estates as he should, by his last Will in writing, limit and appoint or declare.

27th May, 7 Car.

The said Henry Fryer, by his Will, devises the said manor, messuages, and premises to Andrew Burton, Richard Hulett,

John Burton, and Felix Wilson, and their heirs, upon trust that they should, within one year after his death, settle the inheritance of the premises, so as that his Will might be performed. And doth Will that his said trustees should settle £100 for ever, issuing out of all the premises, for the use of the poor of the several parishes of Chiswick, *St. Buttolph's Without Aldersgate*, and Harleton, in the county of Cambridge, whereof the parish of St. Buttolph was principally to be considered.

The sum of £40 per annum, part of the said £100 is by the said Trustees (and two bishops chosen to divide the said £100 per annum amongst the said three parishes) limited and appointed to be paid to the parish of St. Buttolph's.

22nd February, 13 Car.

The said trustees, by their deed enrolled in Chancery, granted the said manor, messuages, and premises to Sir Henry Spiller, John Cordall, Thomas Soames, Thomas Masson the Elder, and Edward Grice, and their heirs, upon trust that they shall pay all and every the rents, annuities, and annual payments as are given, limited, or bequeathed by the Will of the said Henry Fryer to such persons and parishes as are therein expressed.

6th April, 28 Car. 2d.

The following decree was made in Chancery for the settlement of Mr. Fryer's estate, and an additional yearly sum of £10 for ever added to the former guift, as follows:—

Copy of the Decree for the Settlement of Mr. Henry Fryer's Estate.

THIS CAUSE comeing to bee heard before the Right Honourable the Lord High Chancellor of England on the Foure and Twentieth day of February last in the presence of Councill learned on both sides and the case upon which the plaintiffs by their Bill in this Court pray releife being that Henry Fryer late of Saint Buttolphs Without Aldersgate London Esquire was seized in fee of the Mannor of Harleton and certaine lands there with the appurtenances in the County of Cambridge being of the yearly value of £157 10s. 10d. and of diverse messuages or tenements in Aldersgate parish and others in Cripplegate London, being of the yearely value of £331 15s. which in the whole amounts unto the yearely sum of £489 11s. 10d. he did by indenture tripartite the 20th of Aprill 2d Caroli primi, and by fine and recovery and other sufficient conveyance and assurance in law settle the said mannor messuages lands and premises in manner following (viz.) to himself for life and afterwards to such persons and for such estates and uses as hee should appointe by his last Will and that the 20th of May Septino Caroli primi hee made his last Will in writing and thereby bequeathed the said mannor messuages lands and premises and all his estate in Middlesex and all his leases goods chattels cattels jewells plate and household stuffe to Andrew Burton Richard Hewlett John Burton and Felix Wilson their heirs and assigns and appoynted them executors Upon trust that within one yeare after his death they should settle the inheritance of the said premises which were freehold and should estate the rest as far as in them lay that his said Will might be performed And further hee devised to Bridgett his wife besides her thirds amongst other things the use of all his furniture in his house in Chiswicke in the county of Middlesex and in his house in London and a third part of his plate during her life And further devised that the executors should pay unto his brother Thomas tenne pounds per annum at one entire payment to give to such poore as he shall think fitt and desired that the same might be soe settled as that it should be paid for over And he gave unto Mary Woolescott and the heirs of her body lawfully begotten the sum of £100 per annum and alsoe he gave unto the poore of the parish of Saint Buttolph's Aldersgate London and Chiswick in the county of Middlesex and Harleton in the county of Cambridge the sum of £100 per annum and to sundry other persons divers other legacyes and doth afterwards in his Will recomend Aldersgate parish to the particular consideration of his executors because he was borne there and the parish was great and the poore much increased And lastly thereby willed that the surplusage of all his estate whatsoever should bee by his friends and executors and their heirs soe trusted as aforesaid settled and estated to charitable uses for the good of the poore for ever and soone after the making of his said Will dyed without issue which Will the said executors proved and took upon them the execution thereof and that afterwards several differences did arise between the said Dr. John Fryer elder brother of the said testator Henry Fryer and the said executors in relation to the said Will and estate and several suits and proceedings were thereupon comenced and prosecuted between them in the then Court of Wards and Liveryes all which were afterwards by them submitted unto the determination and award of his late Royall Majestie Charles the First who upon examination of the premises was pleased to make and publish his order and award therein and in pursueance thereof the said Henry Fryer's executors by their indenture tripartite bearing date the 22nd February in the 13th yeare of his said late Majestie's reigne reciting his Majestie's said order and otherwise as is therein recited did convey the said mannor lands and premises to certaine trustees and their heirs and assigns for ever in the first place to satisfie all the payments by the said Will and that then they should yearely pay all the rest of the rents and profits of the premises to Dr. John Fryer for life and that after his death the sume of £80 per annum should be towards the perpetuall repair of St. Paul's Church in London and that in the last place all the rest of the profits should be paid to Dr. Fryer's heirs and assigns for ever and that by vertue or colour of the said conveyance the said Dr. John Fryer entered into the possession of the said mannor messuages and estate and during his life received the rents and profits thereof and raised diverse sumes of money for fynes and wood sales and otherwise out of the said estate and afterwards hee the said Dr. John Fryer made his last Will and Testament in writing and thereby devised several parts and parcels of the said lands and premises unto several persons for severall estates and made the defendants John Peacocke and Andrew Matthews executors thereof and gave the defendant Richard Matthews some part of the said lands and premises and about November 1672 died haveing till his death received yearely out of the manor of Harleton £95 16s. 10d. and out of the houses in the parishes of Aldersgate £193 15s. and after his death his said executors alsoe proved his said Will and have ever since received the profits of the said estate to the respective yearely values aforesaid soe that the whole of the said executors yearly receipts were £289 11s. 10d. besides which the said defendant Brigdett received for her thirds out of the said mannors messuages and premises the yearely sume of £200 which makes in all £489 11s. 10d. being the aforesaid yearely vallue of the said estate and the said Dr. John Fryer's executors being allowed out of their said yearely receipts £200 per annum for soe much by them yearely paid or which ought to have been soe paid by the said Henry Fryer's Will (viz.) unto Mary Wallascott or the heirs of her body £100 per annum and unto the said three parishes of *Aldersgate* Chiswick and Harleton £100 per annum there remains as att present cleare surplusage of the said estate the yearely sume of £89 11s. 10d. to be settled and estated to charitable uses for the good of the poore for ever according to the true intent and meaning of the said Henry Fryer's Will over and besides the £200 per annum after the death of the said Bridgett his widdow and as to the said £10 per annum appoynted to bee paid unto Thomas Fryer to be by him distributed as aforesaid in regard it did not appeare that any appointment thereof had beene made and in regard the greatest part of the said donor Henry Fryer's estate doth lye within the parish of Aldersgate and that he had a particular kindnesse for that parish as in and by his said Will is expressed it was by the said Bill prayed the same might be paid to the churchwardens of the said parish from time to time upon the 20th day of

December in every yeare for ever the first payment to be made upon the 20th of December now next ensuing the same to bee distributed by the vicar and churchwardens and common councillmen of the said parishe for the time being amongst twenty poore widdows of the said parish to each of them 10s. a-piece and for want of such poor widdows the said number to be made upp with poore men of the said parish and that the same should be soe distributed as the further charity of the said testator Henry Fryer And further the said Bill sets forth that the said surplusage is devised to the poor in generall within the latitude of which expression are comprehended all the poore in England and soe to construe and apply it would bee to make the said guift to noe signification or effect And further that his now Royall Majestie had beene graciously pleased lately to erect a new Royall foundation in Christ's Hospitall aforesaid for the maintenance of forty poore boys therein to be educated in a mathematicall schoole and instructed in the art of navigation and the whole science of arithmeticke to the end they may bee fitted for the practice of navigation and bee from time to time disposed of in that way and their numbers supplied out of other fitt poore boys in the said hospitall according to the rules and orders of the said new Royall foundation and establishment And that the same is a work of great piety and charity in itselfe and of extraordinary advantage to all his Majestie's dominions and that the settleing and confirming by the decree of this Honourable Court of all the surplusage of the reall and personal estate whatsoever of the said Henry Fryer and also all future improvements of his said reall estate after the death of the said Bridgett the widowe or otherwise howsoever upon the children of the said new Royall foundation would bee a settlement of the said surplusage and future improvements both suitable and agreable to the nature and intent of the said Henry Fryer's Will in all things and also to his Majestie's Royall pleasure for the good of his said new Royall foundation for ever and that the settlement of the said surplusage or any part thereof or of any parto of the said Henry Fryer's estate upon the said Dr. John Fryer his heirs or assigns or in any other manner by the said tripartite indenture or otherwise howsoever is not a settlement thereof to charitable uses for the good of the poore according to the said

Henry Fryer's Will nor ought any such settlement or pretended settlement thereof to prevent or hinder a just and speedy settlement of the same unto such reall and true charitable uses as shall be agreable unto the true intent and meaning of the said Henry Fryer's Will And further that the third part of the said Henry Fryer's plate and all his furniture and goods in and about his house att Chiswicke aforesaid or at London the use whereof was devised to her for life ought alsoe by vertue of his said Will from and after his death to come and be improved to charitable uses for the good of the poore as aforesaid but the said defendants Dr. John Fryer's executors John Peacocke and Andrew Matthews and his legatee Richard Matthews haveing received the rents issues and profits of of the said messuages lands and premises to the aforesaid severall vallues have misimployed and converted the same to their owne uses and the defendant Bridgett haveing gotten the said plate goods and furniture into her custody or power they do by combination endeavour to conceale the true surplusage of the said estate and the reall value thereof and designe to embeazell the said plate goods and furniture and to defraude the severall charitable devises and bequests limitted and intended by the said Will To prevent which and to have a discovery of the true and certaine particulars and vallues of all the reall and personall estate late of the said Henry Fryer and what is the true surplusage thereof and to the end of the same may bee forthwith paid to the said relations for the benefitt of the children of his Majesty's said new Royall foundation and that the said tripartite indenture and all deeds evidences and writings concerning the said estate or the clayme of the said Dr. John Fryer or his said executors or legatee thereunto may be produced and disposed of as to his lordshipp shall seeme meete and that the said defendants John Peacocke Andrew Matthews Richard Matthews and Cornelus Burton may make and execute such conveyance or conveyances or other acts and assurances as shall be fitt for settling and estateing the said mannor lands and premises in such manner as that the particular appointments bequests and charitys given and appointed by the said Henry Fryer's Will may be duely paid and performed And that in particular the said one hundred pounds per annum may be paid to the said three parishes in these proportions (viz.) to Aldersgate forty pounds per annum to Harleton thirty-five pounds per annum and to Chiswicke twenty-five pounds per annum and the ten pounds per annum alsoe paid to the churchwardens of Aldersgate parish to be distributed in manner aforesaid And that all and every the surplusage and future improvements whatsoever of the said estate may be applied and settled to and for the use and benefit of the children of his said Majestie's new Royal foundation in the manner aforesaid or otherwise as to his lordship may seem meete was the scope and effect of the Bill And upon opening of the defendant's Answers whereby the said Henry Fryer's relict insisted that about forty years since she had the use of the said goods and plate for her life and bought the same of the executors and paid for it more than it was worth so long since and the said Doctor's executors received little or nothing thereby out of the said estate since the said Doctor's decease And upon reading the proofes taken in the cause and after long debate thereof his lordship then declared that he would forbear to deliver his final judgment in this cause untill a true state and accomplishment of the testator's Henry Fryer's estate both in possession and reversion were drawne upp and his lordship attended therewith which hath been since done accordingly And his lordship having taken due consideration thereof did appoint this day to consider his finall judgment and determination therein And councell on both sides attending accordingly and the plaintiffs' counsell waveing their former demands for an allowance and satisfaction for the plate goods and furniture and alsoe for the moneys raised by wood sales fynes rents and profits of the said mannor lands and premises and which were actually received by the said defendants the executors and legatee before the exhibiting of the said Bill so as the said estate might be forthwith well and sufficiently conveyed to the said relations for the benefit of the said now Royall foundation and the said tripartite indenture and all other deeds and writings concerning the pretended title or clayme of the said Dr. Fryer or his said executors or legatee or any other claiming under them and all leases and counterparts of leases may be forthwith delivered up to them to be cancelled And that all other conveyances court rolls deeds writings and evidences whatsoever concerning the said Henry Fryer's title claim and interest in and unto the said mannor lands and premises or any part thereof may also be forthwith delivered up to the said relators Whereupon his lordship declared that he had fully considered of this matter and was of opinion having truely acquainted his now Majestie with the true state thereof That where a general charity is given to the poor indefinitely that it is in the power of the King to direct to what poor in particular the same should be applied and that his now Majesty taking notice accordingly that his charity is of that nature he conceived it most fit that all the surplusage of the testator Henry Fryer's estate after his particular bequests hereafter mentioned be discharged should be applied for the benefit of the children in his Majestie's new Royall foundation in Christ's Hospital London and thereupon his lordship conceived it just and reasonable and doth accordingly order and decree that the said defendants the executors John Peacock and Andrew Matthews and Richard Matthews the legatee do convey all and every of their estates right and title respectively in and unto the said mannor and lands in Harleton with its appurtenances thereunto belonging in the said county of Cambrige and also in and unto the said several messuages and tenements in the said parishes of Aldersgate and Cripplegate London and either of them unto the mayor comonalty and cittizens of London governours of the possessions revenues and goods of the hospitalls of Edward King of England the Sixth of Christ Bridwell and St. Thomas the Apostle and their successors for the use and benefit of the children of the said New Royall Foundation for ever freed and discharged for all manner of incumbrances whatsoever suffered or done by them the said defendants John Peacock Andrew Mathews and Richard Mathews respectively as aforesaid or by any other person or persons claiming under them or any of them and that in such manner and forme as Sir Thomas Escourt Knight one of the masters of this Court shall direct and appoint And also that the said executors John Peacock and Andrew Mathews and Richard Mathews the legatee and all and every other person and persons employed by or under them shall forthwith deliver unto the said governers of Christ's Hospital or to such other person as they shall duly authorize or appoint to receive the same the aforesaid tripartite indenture and all the court rolls and other deeds evidences and writings whatsoever which anywise concern the title of the said mannor messuages lands and premises or any of them which they or any of them now have or without suit in law can come by and also all counterparts of leases of the aforesaid premises or any part thereof the aforesaid tripartite indenture and counterparts of leases to be cancelled and the record of the enrollment of the said tripartite indenture to be vacated but nevertheless the said mannor messuages lands and premises are made and so shall from time to time and at all times from henceforth continue and be by force and vertue of this present decree liable unto and stand charged with the dower of the defendant Bridgett Fryer the widdow which was or is assigned to her for her thirds and dower during her life and that she may receive the same in such manner as now she does or by law may and also with the said severall payments of £100 per annum to the said Mary Woollascott and the heirs of her body lawfully begotten according to the said Will and £100 per annum to the aforesaid three parishes in the proportion aforesaid (viz.) to St. Buttolph's Aldersgate £40 per annum to Harleton £35 per annum and to Chiswick £25 per annum and £10 per annum to the poor of Aldersgate as an additionall and further charity of the said Henry Fryer to be annually paid to the churchwardens of the said parish upon the 20th day of December in every year yearly for ever the first payment of the said £10 per annum to be made upon the 20th of December next ensuing and to be yearly distributed by the vicar churchwardens and common councillmen of the said parish amongst twenty poor widdows of that parish to each of them 10s. a-piece and for want of such poor widdows the said number to be made upp with poor men of the said parish and besides the said thirds to the defendant Bridgett and after payment of the aforesaid several sums of £100 per annum and £100 per annum and £10 per annum in manner aforesaid then all and every the surplusage of the rents issues and profits of the said mannor messuage lands and premises with their and overy of their appurtenances at present and to come shall be at all times henceforth and for ever disposed and employed by the said governors and their successors to and for the only use benefit and advantage of the said children of his Majestie's New Royal Foundation in Christ's Hospitall aforesaid and their successors for the time being for ever And that notwithstanding the aforesaid tripartite indenture or the said Will of the said Dr. John Fryer or any conveyances or assurances or other writings whatsoever made or executed by the said Dr. John Fryer or his said executors or legatee or either of them or by any other person or persons whatsoever claiming under the said tripartite indenture or the said Dr. John Fryer or his said executors or legatee on any or either of them they the said governors and 'their successors shall and may at all times hereafter by virtue of this decree peaceably and quietly possess and enjoy all and every the said mannor messuages lands and premises with their appurtenances and receive the rents issues and proffits thereof free and clear from all manner of incumbances whatsoever subject nevertheless unto the aforesaid payments and to the only uses intents and purposes by this decree before limited and appointed and also that all and every the sum and sums of money which since the exhibiting of the said Bill or information have been brought and payed into this Court as part of the rents and profits of the said mannor lands and premises or are unpaid and resting in the hands of any of the tenants of the said premises or any part thereof shall be forthwith paid unto the said governours or to whome they shall authorize and appointe to receive the same to bee imployed for the purpose aforesaid And this Court doth further think fitt and accordingly order and decree that all and every of the tenants of the said messuages lands and premises excepting the tenants of the said Bridgett's parte and dower during her natural life shall upon reasonable demands surrender and deliver upp unto the said governours or to whom they shall authorize and appoint as aforesaid all and every their respective leases of the said premises or any partt thereof to bee cancelled and upon such surrendering thereof the said governours and their successors shall with all convenient speed after make and execute unto each of the tenants so surrendering a new lease of the premises at and under the yearly rents services and covenants and for the remainder of the term of years formerly granted to him her or them in and by such surrendred lease then to come and unexpired and this Court doth likewise think fit and accordingly order and decree that the said defendants yielding obedience unto and performing of this decree according to the true intent thereof that then they and every of them respectively for ever hereafter shall be and by vertue hereof are and is clearly acquited and discharged of and from all further and other accounts claims or demands whatsoever for or in respect of any part or parcell of the said Henry Fryer's reall and personal estate by the said relators in this cause claiming or any wayes controverted of and from all manner of further costs charges and expences whatsoever touching or concerning the same &c.

        Per HENRY DEYNISH.
Copia Vera E.J.   Deput Regr.
 Per JOHN KNIGHT.

OBSERVATIONS.

This Gift is distributed annually, in January or February, to twenty poor Widows, in sums of **£2 10s.** *to each, such Widows being selected by the Fryer's Gift Committee, which Committee consists of the Minister, the Churchwardens, and the Common Council for the Parish.*

It would appear, from the above documents, that the sum of **£40** *per annum was the original value of the Gift, but by the Decree in Chancery before set forth, an additional sum of* **£10** *was ordered to be paid to this Parish, which sum of* **£50** *is now regularly received from the Governors of Christ's Hospital, and distributed as aforesaid.*

SIR HENRY ANDERSON'S GIFT.

In a very old Record Book in the Church the following entry appears.

27th Nov. 4th Car. 2nd.

"Anderson gives Fiftie pounds to buy Land to raise Twelve pence by the week for Bread to be distributed every Sunday."

And upon further search a copy of the following Deed of Covenant was discovered, viz :—

THIS INDENTURE Triptite made the seaven-and-twentyth daye of November in the fourth yeare of the Raigne of our Soveraigne Lorde Charles by the grace of God of England Scotland France and Ireland Kinge Defender of the fayth &c A.D. 1628 between Sir Richard Anderson of Pendley in the countie of Hertford Knight sonne and heire and also sole executor of the last Will and testament of Sir Henry Anderson Knight late Alderman of the cittie of London deceased of the one parte Sir Henry Yelverton Knight one of his Maties Justices of his Court of Comon Pleas William Hakewill of Lincolnes Inne in the countie of Middlesex Esquier Justiman Povey Esquier one of the auditors of his Maties revennewes parishioners of the parishe of St Botolphes without Aldersgate London of the seconde parte and Thomas Booth Clerke now Minister or Vicar of the saide parishe Church of St Botolphes and Anthony Jerman and Helham Rodes nowe Churchwardens of the saide parishe Church of the thirde parte Whereas the saide Sir Henry Anderson Knight did heretofore by his last Will and testament give and bequeath the some of £50 of lawful money of England towards the building of a newe Conduit in Aldersgate Street in the said parish of St Botolphes soe as the same Conduit were there built within seven yeares next after the death of the saide Sir Henry Anderson as by the saide Will more at large appeareth which saide newe Conduit was not built within the saide seaven yeares nor is built at this daye and soe the said legacy is not due nor payable by the saide executor of the saide Will.

Nevertheless this presente Indenture witnesseth that the saide Sir Richard Anderson having a respect of his saide father's pious and charitable intents by his saide Will and tendringe and charitably wishinge the good and reliefe of the poore people of the said parish of St Botolphes without Aldersgate hath of his charitie and free guifte given paide and delivered the daye and yeare above written unto the said Minister or Viccar and Churchwardens of the saide parishe in the presence and with the approbation of the saide Sir Henry Yelverton William Hakewill and Justiman Povey parishioners of the saide parishe the some of £50 of lawfull money of England to the intent and purpose that therewith with the consent of the saide Sir Henry Yelverton William Hakewill and Justiman Povey and their heires and upon notice thereof given to the saide Sir Richard Anderson and his heirs landes tenements rentes or hereditaments in fee simple shall be purchased to the best advantage within one year nowe next ensuinge for the benefitt reliefe and maintenance of the poore people of the saide parishe The inheritance of which saide landes tenements rentes or hereditaments so to be purchased shall be estated and settled in Feofees or Grantees with the consent of the saide Sir Henry Yelverton William Hakewill and Justiman Povey and their heirs for the use of the saide poore to the intent that out of the revenewes thereof twelve pence may be weekly for ever distributed in bread every Sundaye throughoute the yeare in the saide Church to twelve poore inhabitants in the saide parishe at the discretion of the saide Viccar and Churchwardens and their successors or any two of them and that if any overplus remaine of the Revenewes thereof after the saide weekly distribution made that the same overplus shall goe in augmentation of the said bread to be distributed to more poore people there weekly as aforesaide And that until the said landes tenements rentes or hereditaments shall be soe purchased and estated The said fifty pounds shall be from tyme to tyme ymployed with lyke consent as aforesaide and the increase and profitt thereof shall likewise be from tyme to tyme ymployed upon the same weekly distribution of bread everie Sundaye throughoute the yeare as aforesaid towards the reliefe of the saide poore people of the saide parishe And the saide Minister or Viccar and Churchwardens of the saide parishe for themselves severally and for their severall successors Ministers or Viccars and Churchwardens of the saide parishe doe covenante promise and grante to and with the saide Sir Richard Anderson and his heires by these presents that with the said £50 landes tenementes rents or hereditaments in fee simple shall be purchased to the best advantage to the use aforesaid within one yeare now next ensuinge and alsoe settled and assured with such consent and notice as aforesaid And that untill the saide lands tenements rentes or hereditaments shall be purchased and estated as aforesaid the saide £50 shall be employed with consent as aforesaid and that both the profitt and increase of the said £50 until the saide landes tenements rentes or hereditaments shall be purchased and the revennewe of the said landes tenements rentes or hereditaments shall be purchased and estated as aforesaid shall be yearly from tyme to tyme for ever hereafter converted bestowed and whollie imployed to the best and only benefitt behoofe reliefe and maintenance of the poore people of the saide parishe of St Botolphes without Aldersgate London in manner aforesaid and not otherwise In witness whereof the parties above named to these presente Indentures interchangeably have putt their handes and seales the daye and yeare first above written.

And upon investigating the old Vestry Minutes for the year 1629 on the 20th December, the following entry appears:—

"Fiftie pounds of the Guift of Sir Richard Anderson which was agreed to remayne in Mr. Jarman's hands till land should be purchased with the same, or other order taken. It is now therefore further ordered that the said Mr. Jarman shall pay in the said fiftie pounds into the hands of the now Churchwardens on or before the first day of the next Hillary Term or else give such sufficient security for the payment of the same on or before the Annunciation of our Lady next, in the Vestry."

And on the first day of January 1630, the following appears in the Vestry Minutes of that date :

> "According to a former order of the 20th Decr. last
> "Anthony Jarman did paie in full Vestry the sum of fiftie
> "pounds which is agreed to remaine in the iron chest in the
> "Vestry till it be otherwise disposed of by another order."

Which order does not appear to have been made until the 8th of September 1643, when at a Vestry then held the following appears upon the minutes, viz :—

"It is agreed that fiftie pounds heretofore delivered to Mr. Beale of the guift of Sir Richard Anderson shall be paid to Mr. Jarman in parte of his debt due from this parish, and Mr. Beale to be discharged of his securitie given for the same, and the parishioners are to distribute two-and-fifty shillings per annum in bread amongst the poore (according to the donor's directions) of this parish, which said two-and-fifty shillings is to issue out for ever of the rent of the house late in the tenure of Mr. Thomas Booth."

OBSERVATIONS.

In the Churchwardens accounts for the year 1645-6 *appears the following entry, viz:*

> "Received of Mr. Beale this year for bread
> "given by Mr. Richard Anderson to be dis-   £02 : 12 : 00"
> "tributed weekley to the poor.

While upon the payment side of the account the only entry is as follows:

> "Paid at severall tymes to the poor by
> "groates and otherwise according to the
> "usuall forme and will of the bequests before   £027 : 06 : 08 "
> "mentioned as they are particularly charged

And included in that sum doubtless was the £2 : 12 : 0 above mentioned, no separate disbursement appearing; for the two years following the same is entered separately as the gift of Mr. Anderson, and in the year 1648-9 the following entry appears :

"Paid to the poore of this parish att
"severall tymes for supply of their present   £036 : 11 : 10 "
"necessities.   -   -   -   -   -

And similar entries to this appear in the accounts after this, but I find no further trace of the gift as such. In the accounts for the year 1647-8 the following entry appears as a receipt, viz:

"Received of Mr. Bartholomew Beale
"being Mr. Anderson's Guift,   -   -   £060 : 00 : 00 "

And in the same year on the payment side of the account I find the following:

"To Mr. Smith for bread for the poore
"for Mr. Anderson's Guift   -   -   -   £002 : 12 : 00 "

I find no trace of this gift as a separate gift.

In bye gone times, as far back as can be traced, the Upper Churchwarden or Paymaster received the various gifts and donations as well as the poor rates, and from that fund he paid all money for the general relief of the poor, and other expenses of the parish, without reference to any particular mode of distribution; the fact, however, of distributing bread to the poor, both at the workhouse and as out-door relief, was doubtless at that time considered a sufficient compliance with the Wills of the different donors.

The value of the Gift at the date of bequest was **£50**, in 1647 it would appear to be **£60**, but I have no means of stating the value at March 1865.

This Gift is not distributed now.

JAMES GLASBROOKE'S GIFT.

1653. James Glasbrooke by his Will dated in this year (the precise date does not appear) gave to this parish the sum of £166 : 13 : 4, and upon searching the old Vestry Minutes in the year 1657, I find this entry :

"18th day of August 1657.

"Whereas James Glasbrooke late of the parish of St. Botolph without Aldersgate Esquire deceased, in and by his last Will and Testament (amongst diverse other Legacies therein contained) did give unto three several parishes of this City hereafter mentioned the full sume of five hundred pounds in these or the like words following, (that is to say) " and five hundred pounds more to such uses as follows To the poor of the parish where I now dwell five pounds in bread yearly, five pounds to the poor of St. Gyles yearly in bread, to the poor of St. Sepulchre yearly in bread five pounds, this to bee given every Sabbath day in the Churches" As by the said last Will and Testament bearing date the first day of 1653 due relation being thereunto had itt doth and may appear, and whereas one hundred three score and six pounds thirteen shillings and fourpence parcel of the said sum of five hundred pounds so limited by the said Will and being one full third parte thereof doth accrue and properly come and belonge unto the poor of the parish of St. Botolph without Aldersgate London in which the said James Glasbrooke did in his lifetime and at his death dwell and inhabit which Joan Glasbrooke widow the relict and executrix of the said James Glassbrooke deceased is willing to pay over to the use of the poor of this parish of St. Botolph.

"Now the parishioners of the said parish of St. Botolph being assembled in the Vestry of the said parish Church do agree order direct and appoint that Thomas Turner and John Sherley the now present Churchwardens of this parish doe apply themselves to the said Joan Glasbrooke and demand the said one hundred three score and six pounds thirteen shillings and fourpence of her, being the full thirde parte of the said five-hundred pounds to be used and employed by this parish for the use of their poore for ever according to her late Husband's intention expressed by his last Will and Testament and to give unto her an acquittance and discharge for the payment of the said sume as shee is executrix And the said parishioners of the said parish in their Vestry assembled doth further order direct and appoint that the said money soe by the said Churchwardens received and discharged as is above directed that there shall be yearly for ever paid and given to the poore of this parish as the increasement and benefit of the said legacy the said several sums of money hereafter mentioned, that is to say the sum of five pounds and four shillings every year in bread to be distributed and given to the poore of this parish every Sabbath day in the Church at and by the discretion of the Churchwardens and Overseers of the poore of the parish for ever according to the minde of the Testator expressed in his last Will and Testament and for a further benefit to the said poore of this parish to arise out of the said legacie This Vestry doth alsoe order and agree that there be yearly paid for ever to twenty poore people of this parish twelvepence a piece on the Feast day of St. James the Apostle in every yeare to be alsoe distributed by the Churchwardens and Overseers of the poore and twelve of the most ancient of this parish to be from time to time appointed and chosen in the Vestry where they shall think fitt Alsoe they doe order that out of the said legacie money soe given thirteen shillings and fourpence yearly be given for ever to a Godly pious and learned Minister to preach a sermon on the said Feast day of St. James in every year to celebrate the memory of the said James Glasbrooke for this his pious and charitable guift unto the poore of this parish and to invyte and stirr others upp to doe the like and to followe and bee ledd by so good an example and after the said sermon ended every yeare the poore soe to be appointed for the said charity to be paid and satisfied accordingly And that if any further or other advantage or benefit shall be had or made of or by the said moneys soe given as aforesaid that then such money that shall be overplus and remaining to be annually bestowed on other poore of this parish in and by the discretion of the Churchwardens for the time being and twelve of the most ancient of the said parish as before is directed and this guift soe appointed to bee stand remaine abide and continue perpetuall."

OBSERVATIONS.

The above-mentioned sum of £166 : 13 : 4 *was received by the Churchwardens, Messrs. Turner and Sherley, as appears by the following entry in their accounts for the year* 1657-8

"Recd more as the Gift of Mr. Alderman "Glassbrooke to the poore of this parish   £166 : 13 : 04

From the year 1663 *to* 1690, *both inclusive, it appears by the Churchwarden's accounts that the sum of* £1 : 13 : 4 *was distributed to the poor as the Gift of Mr. James Glassbrooke, but it does not shew in what manner it was distributed, or from what source derived.*

There are no accounts entered from the year 1690 *to* 1714.

In the year 1715 *the Churchwardens received and gave credit for the various gifts, but the only entry as to the distribution thereof is as follows:*

"Paid by discretion to several poor for the "whole year   -   -   -   £99 : 16 : 6

After which period I find no further trace of this gift, or how the £166 : 13 : 4 *was invested, if at all; but in the Churchwardens' accounts for the year* 1658-9, *being the year following the receipt of the gift, this entry appears:*

> " Paid to Dr. Denton for the purchase of
> " the Lease of the Church-house wherein
> " Sir Henry Martin dwelt, and the Lease £746 : 00 : 00
> " of Mr. Woodroffe's house, and of certain
> " Rooms in the Half Moon   -   -

£470 *of which was obtained from the sale of the estate in Essex, which had been purchased by the bequest of Mr. Christopher Tamworth, for full particulars of which see Tamworth's Gift, page* 12.

There is no evidence that I can find which shews where the remainder was derived from, and therefore it can only be assumed that this and other pecuniary gifts to the parish, together with fines for not serving parish offices, formed the balance of the purchase money, and that the income, so long as it was accounted for separately, was obtained from the rent of these premises; and my reason for so thinking is, that in the various accounts in which the gift is mentioned as paid separately, they are perfectly silent as to its receipt.

The value of the gift at the date of bequest was £166 : 13 : 4 *but I have no means of ascertaining the value at March* 1865.

For further observations see Anderson's Gift, page 79.

This gift is not distributed now.

MR. JAMES ACTON'S GIFT.

The following is an extract from the Will of Mr. James Acton, and Deed of Release from Mr. Smith, the then Churchwarden of this parish, to Mr. Acton's executors:

"*Item* Whereas I have lived long in the parish of St. Botolph without Aldersgate London and believe that there are severall poore inhabitants of the said parish that have charges of children and are not able to place them out or dispose of them in some good course of living though unwilling to make the same known for some help and relief unto them in that behalf I do give and bequeath unto the Churchwardens of the said parish for the time being for the purpose aforesaid the sum of fifty pounds of lawful English money to be paid them within one year next after my decease and to be put out by them and their successors for ever to the best profit that may be made thereof and at the end of every five years to place out a child of such poore inhabitants as is before expressed with the benefit which shall in that time be raised thereby."

The Churchwardens executed a Deed of Release to Mr. Acton's executors, which is as follows:—

"Whereas James Acton late of Aldersgate Street London did by his last Will and Testament give and bequeath unto the Churchwardens of the said parish for the time being the sum of fifty pounds to be by them put out for the best profit that may be made thereof and at the end of every five years to place out a child of some poor inhabitant of the said parish with the benefit which shall in that time be raised thereby as by the said Will more fully appears Now know all men by these presents that we

Henry Smith and John Wilson inhabitants and Churchwardens of the said parish have the day of the date of these presents had and received of William Brand Esq. John Ayleworth and Henry Byne Gentlemen executors of the last Will and Testament of the said James Acton by the hands of the said John Ayleworth the said sum of fifty pounds of lawful money of England in full of the said legacy and in consideration thereof we do by these presents for us and our successors acquit release and discharge the said William Brand John Ayleworth and Henry Byne and every of them their and every of their executors and administrators of and from the said legacy sum and sums of money and all other demands by virtue of the said Will of the said James Acton In witness whereof we have hereunto set our hands and seals this 29th day of May 1668.

"HENRY SMITH.

"Sealed and delivered by the above-named Henry Smith in the presence of } THOMAS WEARY. JOHN PHILLIPS."

"Adam Fenner promised to be the first person placed out by Mr. Acton's gift."

OBSERVATIONS.

Upon searching the Vestry Minutes for the year 1668 *I find that the above documents are entered there also.*

At a Vestry held on the 28th October, 1668, *I find the following:*

"Ordered that Mr. Acton's money and the fines be put forth "for the best advantage."

And at a Vestry held on the 1st February, 1668, *the following minute appears:*

"Be it remembered that Mr. Henry Smith Churchwarden "received Fifty pounds of Mr. James Acton's money and "also Fifty pounds more of Fines for Offices which the several Common Councilmen received and payed

"All which moneys was put out to the best advantage by Mr. Thos. Wearye January 28th 1668-9 as appears by a Bond dated the same day and year above written

"Which Bond was delivered to Mr. Henry Smith, Churchwarden by the Vestrymen February 1st 1668-9

"Witness JAMES CLIFFORD."

Upon searching the Vestry Minutes still further, I find that at a Vestry held on the 6th day of August, 1673, the following:

"It is this day likewise ordered that Mr. Littlebury, Churchwarden, doe pay unto Widd. Turner the sum of £15 for ye putting forth apprentice of Adam Fenner being the guift of Mr. James Acton for ye putting forth of a boy once in 5 years the said Adam being the first disposed of by the said Guift."

In the Churchwardens' account for the year 1673-4 I find no entry as to the receipt of Mr. Acton's gift, but this entry appears:

"Paid to Elizth Turner for Adam Fenner put out Apprentice by order of Vestry being the Guift of Mr James Acton - - } £015 : 00 : 00"

At another Vestry held on the 18th day of October, 1678, the following minute appears:

"Ordered that Gooddy Greene's sonne be put forth Apprentice out of the profit and interest of the £50 Gift by Mr James Acton deceased according to the Will of the Donor."

On searching the Churchwardens' accounts for that and subsequent years, I find no mention of the above Order of Vestry having been carried out, neither can I discover any further trace of the gift after that date.

The value of the Gift at the date of bequest was **£50**, but I have no means of ascertaining the value at March 1865.

This Gift is not distributed at the present time.

MR. ROBERT LOGGINS' GIFT.

In the last Will and Testament of Robert Loggins is contained a clause in these words following, viz:

"Item I give and bequeath the sum of £50 to the use of St. Buttolph without Aldersgate London to the intent that the Churchwardens and overseers of the poor of the said parish shall from time to time for ever dispose and employ the increase and produce of the said £50 towards the relief of thirty of the most poorest and indigent inhabitants of the said parish which I would have done as followeth, viz. That each and everyone of the said thirty poore have one twopenny loaf of bread a piece and the residue in money to be apportioned and distributed in such manner as the wants and necessities of the said poor in the judgment and opinion of the said Churchwardens and Overseers of the poor (for the time being) or any three of them shall be and approve yet so that no one of them shall have less than one shilling for his or her dole or proportion And my Will is that the bread be set upon some shelfe in some conspicuous place in the said Church to be erected and sett up by my executors for the better prevention of any fallacy or wrong to the said poor and the same to be distributed yearly and every year for ever on the nine-and-twentieth day of May being the day of the birth and happy return of our most gracious King Charles the Second after his expulsion and many years absence out of this Kingdom."

OBSERVATIONS.

The above is extracted from an old Record Book in the Church, and on examining the Churchwardens' (Messrs. Nicholas Purse and

Thomas Williams) accounts for the year 1670 and 1671, this item appears :

"Received of Mr. Loggins being his Father's Guift to the Poore £50 and for interest £2 : 10 : 0 in toto - - - £052 : 10 : 0"

And upon searching the Minutes of Vestry I find, at a Meeting held on the 11th August, 1671, the following Resolution or Order :

"It is also Ordered that the Fifty pounds the Gift of Mr. Robert Loggins deceased be put into the hands of Mr. Portman at interest for the use of the Poore and that a Bond be therefore taken for the use of the parish."

Which was accordingly done, and in the Churchwardens' accounts for the year 1672 the following entry appears :

"Received of Mr. Portman for the interest of £150 - - - - - - £009 : 00 : 00"

I have no means of ascertaining what the £150 so put into Mr. Portman's hands consisted of, but entries as to the receipt of the interest similar to the above are made in the accounts each year until the year 1678, in which year, on the 30th May, at a Vestry Meeting then held, it is ordered as follows :

"Ordered that an Assignment be taken out in the Exchequer for the money due from Mr. Portman to this parish according to Counsell in the names of the Trustees hereafter mentioned their heirs and assigns for the use of the poor of the parish.

"Memorand : That the same day the Vestry has elected and chosen the persons hereunder named to be Trustees for the use aforesaid, viz.

"TRUSTEES.

" THOMAS WEARY, ESQ.	ROBERT SCOTT
" ROBERT LITTLEBURY	RICHARD GREENS
" JOHN FISH	SAMUEL MABBS"

Which Order appears to have been complied with, and the interest regularly received up to the year 1690.

On the payment side of the various accounts from 1672 *to* 1690, *both inclusive, the sum of* £3 *is stated to have been distributed to the poor as Mr. Loggins' gift, but it does not appear in what manner, or where received from.*

There are no accounts entered from 1690 *to* 1714, *and I find no further trace of this gift being distributed as such.*

See also observations as to Anderson's Gift, page 79.

The value of the Gift at the date of bequest was £50, *and on its receipt with interest* **£52 : 10 : 0,** *but its value at March* 1865 *I have no means of ascertaining.*

It is not distributed now.

MR. JOHN MYNN'S GIFT.

In the last Will and Testament of Mr. John Mynn late citizen and Grocer of London deceased bearing date the 18th day of October Anno Domini 1670 (amongst other things) is contained as followeth: "I give and bequeath to the poor of St. Buttolph without Aldersgate London the sum of £50 in money to be laid out by the Vestrymen of the said parish for the best advantage and benefit of the poor thereof in such manner as the same Vestrymen shall in their discretion seem meet."

Which said sum of £50 was paid into the hands of Mr. John Fish, Churchwarden, A.D. 1676.

OBSERVATIONS.

The above extract appears in a very old book in the Church, and upon searching the old Vestry Minute Book, at a Vestry held on the 13th November, 1676, the following Order is entered:

> "Ordered That Mr. Fish the present Churchwarden do
> "receive of Mr. Keeling the Executor of the last Will and
> "Testament of Mr. John Mynn deceased the sum of Fifty
> "pounds to the use of the parish being a Legacy given by
> "the said Will of the said John Mynn."

And upon investigating the accounts of Messrs. Hyde and Fish, Churchwardens for the year 1676, the following entry appears:

> "Received of Mr. Keeling the Executor
> "of Mr. John Mynn deceased being a Legacy   £050 : 00 : 00 "
> "by him left to the poore of this parish

I find no further trace of the Gift, or how it was applied. See also observations as to Anderson's Gift, page 79.

The value of the Gift at the date of bequest was **£50** *What its value was at March 1865 I have no means of ascertaining.*

MR. WILLIAM THORNBURY'S GIFT.

In searching through the old Vestry Minutes for the year 1679, at a Vestry Meeting held on the 3rd day of September in that year, the following Order appears, viz.

"Ordered that the Upper Churchwardens doe receive the "Guift of Mr. Thornbury deceased being £25 And that "there bee £1 : 5 : 0 a year distributed to the poore of this "parish for ever on such day as the executor shall appointe "and that the Houses demised to Mr. Turner shall be "chargeable with the payment thereof."

And upon searching the Churchwardens' Accounts for the year 1679-80 the following entry appears :

"Received of the Executor of Mr. William "Thornbury being soe much by him left to £25 : 00 : 00" "the poore of this parish - - -

And in the Accounts for the year 1680-81 the sum of £5 appears to have been distributed to the poor as Mr. William Thornbury's Gift, but it does not say in what manner; and I find, in the years 1682-3 the sum of £1 : 5 : 0 is distributed as Mr. Thornbury's Gift: from this time I find no further trace of this Gift.

OBSERVATIONS.

This Gift was not distributed after the year 1683, *but I have no means of ascertaining the reason of the same being discontinued.*

In the Churchwardens' accounts for the year 1683 *the following appears as a receipt :*

"Also with one year's rent of Mr. Thomas
"Turner for the Blackhorse and Blackhorse } £20 : 00 : 00 "
"Alley in Aldersgate Street - -

"Which property is specially charged as above with the
"payment of this Gift."

This property is still in the possession of the parish, and is now known as 141, *Aldersgate Street; for full particulars see copy of the Trust Deed.*

The value of the Gift at the date of bequest was **£25,** *but I have no means of giving the value at March* 1865.

See also observations on Anderson's Gift, page 79.

It is not distributed now.

MR. NICHOLAS GODWIN'S GIFT.

In the last Will and Testament of the above Donor, dated the 6th December, 1695, is the following, viz.:

"*Item* My Will is that my personall estate after my debts and funeral charges shall be paid and satisfied to be divided into three equal parts or shares according to the custom of the City of London One full and equal third part or share thereof I give unto my loving wife Elizabeth Godwin for her part according to the said custom one other third part thereof I give and bequeath unto such child or children as I shall have living at the time of my decease or wherewith my wife shall be then enciente or with child and out of the other third part in my owne disposall according to the custom of the said City I give and bequeath the legacie following viz. I give and bequeath to my sister Jane Applegate Two hundred pounds *Item* I give unto the Churchwardens of the the parish of St. Botolph without Aldersgate London for the time being the sum of fifty pounds for the purchasing of land and inheritance for ever of the value of fifty shillings per annum which I Will shall be settled upon twelve good and sufficient parishioners of the said parish to be chosen by a Vestry and their heirs in trust to be laid out in a dozen of penny loaves weekly to be distributed to twelve poor people of the said parish on every Sabbath day for ever And upon further trust that when all but four of the said Trustees shall be dead the survivors of them shall convey the said lands soe to be purchased as aforesaid to twelve other good and sufficient parishioners of the said parish to be chosen by a Vestry and their heirs in trust for the purpose aforesaid and soe from time to time for ever and my Will is that the charges of the conveyance upon the purchase and first settlement of the said land upon Trustees to the uses aforesaid shall be paid out of my estate and that until such purchase shall be made my Will is that the said bread shall be distributed by and out of the interest of the said fifty pounds.

OBSERVATIONS.

This Gift appears to have been bequeathed in the year 1695.

On carefully searching the Vestry Minutes, at a Vestry held on the 9th day of March, 1702, *I find the following order, viz.:*

"Ordered that the 12d. per week for bread being the guift of Mr. Nicholas Godwin be from henceforth for ever paid out of the rents and profits of the freehold part of the above said premises lett to Captain William Smith as above said."

There being no Churchwardens' accounts from the year 1690 *to* 1714, *and nothing further appearing on the Minutes, I have no other means of ascertaining anything more relating to the Gift.*

The property above mentioned to be let to Captain Smith, and which is charged with this Gift, is still in our possession, and is now known as 129, *Aldersgate Street.*

For full particulars see copy of Trust Deed.

Its value at the date of bequest was **£2 : 10s.** *per annum, and being a charge upon the above property I presume it would be of the same value at March* 1865.

It is not distributed now.

BUDE'S GIFT.

Memorand. That we Roger Wilson Citizen and Merchant Tailor of London late Churchwarden of the parish of St. Buttolphe without Aldersgate London and William Stokes Citizen Leather-seller of London now Churchwarden of the said parish doe acknowledge ourselves to have received att and before the daie of the date hereof of William Wase gentleman Executor of the last Will and Testament of Richard Bude Esquire deceased the whole sum of thirtie pounds of lawful English money viz. to the said Roger Wilson £11 : 15 : 4 hereof A.D. 1630 within the tyme of my Churchwardenship and to the said William Stokes £18 : 4 : 8 residue on the daie of the date hereof in full payment of the said thirtie pounds which was given by the said Richard Bude in his lifetyme for stock to be yearly employed by the Churchwardens of the said parish for the tyme being for to buy coles at the best rate and to sell them to the poore of the said parish at the cheapest rate they may soe as the said thirtie pounds may for ever remayne as a stocke to be yearly bestowed in coles to the poor of the said parish In witness whereof we have hereunto putt our hands and seals the six-and-twentieth day of May in the eighth year of the raigne of our Sovereign Lord Charles by the Grace of God of England Scotland France and Ireland King defender of the faith &c. A.D. 1632.

OBSERVATIONS.

The above appears entered in the Vestry Minutes for the year 1632, *there being no Churchwardens' accounts until the year* 1637-8; *I find no further mention of this gift as such, but in the Churchwardens' accounts for the year* 1640 *this entry appears*

"Received for 17 Chaldron of Coales
"sold to the poore at five pence per bushell, } £009 : 10 : 00"

Also a similar entry for 1642 *and several years after, but I have no means of ascertaining whether this was a compliance with the above gift or not, nothing appearing in the Vestry Minutes that gives any such information.*

The value at the date of bequest was **£30**, *but I cannot state the value at March* 1865.

It is not acted upon at the present time.

MRS. KATHERINE PURDEN'S GIFT.

"Katherine Purdyn of this Parish gave unto the poor thereof £10 for which there is ordered as before by the same Vestry to be paid yearly untill &c. - - - - - - } 20s."

OBSERVATIONS

The above memorandum is bound in the front of the first of the old Vestry Minutes Books commencing 1601, and on searching at Doctors' Commons for the Will of the above benefactress to the parish, I obtained the following extract, viz:

[Extracted from the Principal Registry of Her Majesty's Court of Probate.]

"In the Prerogative Court of Canterbury.

"In the Will of Katherine Purden late of the parishe of St. Butolphes withoute Aldersgate London spinster deceased dated 3rd March 1611 is as follows:

"I give to the poore of the parishe of St. Butolphes withoute Aldersgate London to be bestowed in bread the daye after my buriall twenty shillings.

"Item. I give to the poore of the parishe of St. Butolphes
"without Aldersgate foresaid tenne poundes tenne shillings
"to be distributed to the poorest and anncientest sorte of
"people there at the appointment and discretion as well of
"the Churchwardens and Minister of the same Church as
"of myne Executor and Overseer hereafter named.

And upon reading further through the minutes at a Vestry held on the 22nd March, 1620, *the following appears*:

"Whereas there has lately beene disbursed and taken
"out of monies which were given unto the reliefe of the
"poore viz. £20 of Mrs Roberts wife of Tedder Roberts
"late deceased who in his last Will and Testament be-
"queathed the same for the use of the said poore and of Mr.
"Wotton executor for Katherine Purdyn late of this parish
"£10 who in her last Will and Testament bequeathed the
"same for the use of the said poore and £10 taken from the
"stock of the said poore All which moneyes went to the
"repairing of the frame and belles of the Church of St.
"Buttolphes Be it remembered it is agreed at a Vestrie
"holden the day and year above written by the Vestrymen
"of the said parish that in consideration of these moneyes
"of the poore the said poore of the parish shall have £3
"per annum paid unto them oute of the profit of bells
"coming to the parish upon the 22nd day of November
"to be paid by every Churchwarden for the tyme
"being from tyme to tyme until the said £40 be repaid
"unto the poore boxe Also it is consented and agreed upon
"by consent aforesaid that the wife of Tedder Roberts shall
"have soe long as she liveth the appointment of 10 poore
"people to receive parte of the contribution as it shall be
"thought fitt by the distributors Alsoe that Mr. Wotton
"shall have the nomination of 4 persons in like sort."

There are no Churchwardens' accounts entered until the year 1637, *when I find the following entry*:

"Perpetually to be yearly distributed to the poore of the
"parish out of the bequests of the several persons hereafter
"mentioned, viz. of

" The Lady Packington	004	13	04
" Mr. John Morley	005	00	00
" Mr. John Conyers	005	00	00
" Mr. Richard Osmotherlaw	005	00	00
" Mr. Roger Taylor	005	00	00
" Mrs. Dane for Faggotts	000	10	00
" Mr. Stephen Scudamore for Faggots	001	00	00
" Mrs. Margaret Adams	000	10	00
" Mr. Henry Leake	000	06	00
" Mrs. Hibbens	005	00	00
" Mr. Westwood	002	10	00
" Mr. Crippes	001	00	00
" Mr. Court	000	14	00
" Mr. Medcalfe	000	14	00
" Mrs. Jane Jenkyns	002	13	04
" Mr. Tedder Roberts	002	00	00
" Mrs. Katherine Purden	001	00	00
" Received of Mr. Beale this year for " Bread given by Mr. Richard " Anderson to be distributed " weekly to the poore	002	12	00
" Mr. Philip Holman	002	00	00
" Mr. Kempster	000	13	04
" Mr. Gadbury	004	06	08
" Mr. Frier	040	00	00

As to each of these Gifts all information that can be obtained will be given under their respective names.

I find similar entries as to this Gift made each year in the accounts until the year 1640. *There are no accounts entered for the year* 1641-2, *neither do I find any further mention of the Gift.*

Its value at the date of bequest was **£11 10s.**, *but I have no means of ascertaining the value at March* 1865, *or why the distribution was discontinued.*

It is not distributed now.

MR. TEDDER ROBERTS' GIFT.

"Tedder Roberts of this parish Vintner gave unto the poore thereof £20 and it is ordered at a Vestry held on the 22nd March 1620 that there shall be paid yearly until it be bestowed upon some perpetuity - . - - - } 40s."

OBSERVATIONS.

The above entry is also bound in front of the first Vestry Minute Book bearing date 1601, *and after searching at Doctors' Commons, and finding there the original Will, I obtained this extract therefrom, viz.*:

[Extracted from the Principal Registry of Her Majesty's Court of Probate.]

"In the Prerogative Court of Canterbury.

"In the Will of Tedder Roberts late citizen and "vintner of London deceased dated 1st December "1618 is as follows :—

"Item. I give and bequeath to the poore of the parish of "St. Buttolphs without Aldersgate London the some of "twentie pounds of lawfull money of England to be paid "to the Churchwardens of the said Parishe to the use of "the said poore within six months next after my decease to "be bestowed and ymployed towards the yearely mainte-"nance and reliefe of the poore of the said parish."

For further observations see Mrs. Katherine Purden's Gift, page 98, *as they apply to this one in precisely the same manner.*

It is not distributed now.

Its value at the date of bequest was **£20**, *I cannot give the value at March* 1865.

MR. HUMFRIE WESTWOOD'S GIFT.

Also in front of the Old Vestry Minutes, 1601, I find the following entry, viz.:

"Humfrie Westwood gouldsmith gave by his last Will to
"the poore of this parish payable to ye Churchwardens at
"Michaelmas or Lady daye 50s. for and during all ye time
"that he hath in the lease of the tenements in Maydenhead
"Alley.

OBSERVATIONS.

Not having succeeded in ascertaining for what purpose this gift was to be applied, I searched at Doctors' Commons for the Will, and when found I obtained the following extract therefrom, namely:

[Extracted from the Principal Registry of Her Majesty's Court of Probate.

"In the Prerogative Court of Canterbury.

"In the Will of Humfrie Westwood late citizen
"and goldsmith of London deceased dated 20th
"May 1622 is as follows:—

"Item. I will and bequeathe to the Churchwardens of
"the said parishe of St. Buttolphes without Aldersgate to
"be distributed to and amongst the poore of the same
"parishe to be yssuing out of the rentes and profittes of the

"tenements leased by Mr. Taylor as aforesaide unto me for
"and duringe the residue of the tearme of years thereby
"granted one annuitie or yearely some of fiftie shillinges to
"be paide to the saide Churchwardens of the saide parishe
"at twoe times in the yeare that is to say at the feastes of
"St. Michaell the Archangell and the Annunciacion of our
"Ladye St. Mary the Virgin or within twentie daies nex
"ensuinge everie of the saide feastes days the first payment
"thereof to begin at the feaste of St. Michaell the Arch-
"angell which shall nexte happen after my decease."

I have not been able to ascertain the interest of Mr. Westwood in the property above referred to.

It will be seen by reference to page 98, that in the first Church-wardens' account that £2 : 10 : 0 was distributed as the Gift of Mr. Westwood, but it does not say in what manner, and similar entries are found for several years after, when they cease, and I find no further trace of the Gift. Its value at bequest would appear to be **£2 : 10 : 0** *per annum, but I cannot state its value (if anything) at March, 1865.*

PHILLIP HOLEMAN'S GIFT.

In the front of the Old Vestry Minutes before referred to, the following entry appears, viz.:

"Phillipp Holeman of Broad Street London giveth to ye "poore of this parishe the some of 40s. to be distributed by "the Churchwardens at their discreation about New Yeare's "Tide which is at his pleasure in respect of his deliverance "from being murthered by treacherous persons set in ye "corner house at Maydenhead Alley in Aldersgate Street "and was relieved by one of yo poore of this parishe sitting "at ye dore by chance.

OBSERVATIONS.

This Gift was received and distributed from the year 1637 *(if not before) up to* 1643, *when it appears to have ceased for two years, and then is renewed again and continued to be distributed until the year* 1673, *when the following entry appears in the Churchwardens' accounts, viz.:*

"The Guift of Phillipp Holman Esqre due for the yeare "ending as above said nil for that the said Phillipp Holman "paide the said Guift during pleasure and being since "deceased nothing ought to be charged in futuro."

The value of the Gift was £2 *per annum while received, but on the death of the Donor ceased.*

JANE JENKYN'S or GIANKIN'S GIFT.

This Gift is also entered in front of the old Vestry Minutes before mentioned, and is as follows, viz.:

> "A Gentleman unknown hath given towardes the building of the fyve newe shoppes at the East End of the Church the some of £36 to the end that out of the rentes of the said five shops four markes might be yearely collected and distributed in this manner for the time viz.:
>
> "To the poore of this parish on Midsummer daie in the morning to 40 of them yearelie 40s. To the Minister of this parish for a sermon to be on that day 10s.
>
> "To the Clarke and Sexton 3s. 4d.
>
> "In all yearelie every yeare 53s. 4d.

OBSERVATIONS.

It appears to have been afterwards discovered that the Gift was from Jane Jenkins, as the following is written in the margin opposite the above, viz:

> "Jane ye daughter of Roger and Jane Giankins gave this Gift to be distributed upon Midsummer day beinge her birth day"

In the first Churchwardens' accounts 1637, this Gift was distributed as Jane Jenkyn's Gift, but it does not say in what manner.

The rent then received for the five shops appears to have been £6 : 13s. 4d. as the following entry in the Churchwardens' accounts for the year 1637 shews, viz.:

> "And with a years rent for five shopps
> "at the Churchyard in Aldersgate Street
> "demised to William Yearsley Peter
> "Blagrane and Henry Pauncefoote } £006 13 04"

I have no means of ascertaining the precise date of this Gift save that it was before 1637.

The value of a marke was 13s. 4d.

The rents of the said shops were regularly received, and this Gift distributed yearly until the year 1690, *after which there are no accounts until the year* 1714, *when the same ceases to be distributed as a separate Gift.*

For further observations see Anderson's Gift, page 79.

The rent of the shops in the year 1690 *was* £20 *which rent sometimes a little more or less continued to be received until the year* 1733, *when the following Order of Vestry was made, viz.:*

> "At a Committee of Vestry held 10th December 1733
> "Ordered that Churchwardens Hopkins and Roades do
> "pull down the shops at the East end of the Church and
> "that they do pave the same with square stone and put
> "down good large posts of oak (with the tops capt) at the
> "full extent of the ground whereon the shops stood"

After which I find no further trace of this Gift.

Its value while the rents of the shops were received was £2:13:4 *per annum, but I cannot state the value at March* 1865.

It is not distributed now.

MR. WILLIAM COURT'S GIFT.

The following is also entered in front of the old Vestry Minutes before mentioned, viz:

> "William Court late of this parish gentleman deceased gave unto the poore of this parish £10 which was likewise disbursed in the building of the said five shops and for which out of the rents of the said shops there is yearly to be answered upon St. Peter's day to fourteen poor people for ever 14s.

OBSERVATIONS.

By the Churchwardens' accounts this Gift appears to have been distributed separately for about four years, after which I find no further trace of it.

For further observations see Jane Jenkyn's Gift, page 103.

Its value at the date of bequest, which was before 1637, was **£10**, *but I cannot tell the value at March 1865, nor the precise date of the Gift.*

See also observations on Anderson's Gift, page 79.

MR. THOMAS METCALFE'S GIFT.

This Gift is also mentioned in front of the old Vestry Minutes, viz :

"Thomas Metcalfe late of this parish gave unto the poore "thereof £10 which was likewise disbursed in the building "of the said five shops and for which there is yearly to be "answered upon All Saints Day to fourteen poor people "for ever 14s."

OBSERVATIONS.

This Gift was distributed as Thomas Metcalfe's Gift for many years, when it ceases, the same as the previous Gift, to be mentioned separately.

For further observations see Jane Jenkyn's Gift, which applies to this in the same manner, page 103.

See also observations on Anderson's Gift, page 79.

The value of the Gift at the date of bequest was **£10** *but I cannot state the value at March,* 1865, *or the precise date of the Gift save that it was prior to* 1637.

It is not distributed now.

MR. GEORGE ALLINGTON,
SIR JAMES ALTHAM, Knight,
AND
MR. JOHN WOTTON'S GIFTS.

An account of these Gifts is also bound in front of the old Vestry Minutes, and is as follows, viz. :

"GEORGE ALLINGTON sendeth to be distributed to the poore of this parish every yeare at Xmas the sum of 40s. at his pleasure and by the discretion of ye Churchwardens for the tyme beeinge to dispose the same.

"JAMES ALTHAM, KNIGHT, sendeth at his pleasure yearely the sum of 40s. about Candlemas to be distributed at the discreation of the Mynister and Churchwardens to the poore of this said parish.

"JOHN WOTTON gentleman giveth at his pleasure to the poore of this parish 30s. to be distributed at the discreation of the Mynister and Churchwardens yearly."

OBSERVATIONS.

The above Gifts being at the will and pleasure of the respective Donors, ceased with their lives.

I have no means whatever of giving the dates of these Gifts, or how they were appropriated.

WILLIAM SWAYNE'S GIFT.

In front of the Vestry Minutes before alluded to the following extract appears, viz. :

"WILLIAM SWAYNE late of this parish gentleman deceased gave unto the poore of the same £20 to the end that there might be distributed amongst them yearly for ever upon All Saints Day 26s. 8d.

OBSERVATIONS.

There is no date to this Gift, nor can I find any further trace of it. It is not distributed now.

MR. HENRY LEAKE'S GIFT.

In front of the old Vestry Minutes (1601), the following appears:

> "HENRY LEAKE late of the parish of St. Olave in the Borough of Southwark in the County of Surrey deceased gave unto parishes within the liberties of London (whereof this parish is one) payable in or about the month of Aprill to the Churchwardens for the time being to the use of the poore yearely every yeare the some of 6s. or 6s. 8d. at the discretion of the Churchwardens of St. Olaves who pay the same."

OBSERVATIONS.

In searching through the old Records I find this entry, viz.:

> "Henry Leake appointed 6s. or 6s. 8d. to be paid by the Churchwardens of the parish of St. Olave's in Southwarke to the Churchwardens of this parish in or about the month of April, in every year for the use of the poore of this parish. } VIs. VIIId."

Also the following note:

> "Note—A demand has been made of the arrears due to this parish on account of the above Gift but the parish of St. Olave refuse to pay anything till the title of this parish to the above claim is properly ascertained.
>
> "By Iliff's History of Gifts to this parish Henry Leake died in the year 1715."

There evidently is an error in this last paragraph, as upon reference to the Churchwardens' accounts for the year 1637 this Gift is mentioned as having been distributed.

There are no accounts for 1640-41.

In the accounts for 1642 I find the following entry as a receipt:

"Mr. Henry Leake paid by the Church-
"wardens of St. Olave's Southwark.   } 000 : 06 : 00"

I find no other mention of this Gift until the year 1648, when 11s. 10d. appears to have been received and distributed, after which I find no further trace of the Gift.

I have searched diligently for a long time at Doctors' Commons for the Will, first in the General Books, then in the Surrey Calendars, and last of all in Books for the Consistory Court of London, from 1600 to 1800, and have seen a great many Wills of persons of the name of Henry Leake, but not been so fortunate as to find the right one.

It will be seen above that in one place he is said to have appointed the Gift. If this is so it might have been done by Deed, and I should then have no means of tracing it.

I am still continuing my searches as to this Gift.

Its value at bequest or appointment would appear to be **6s.** per year, but its value at March 1865 I am at present unable to state.

The Perpetual Annuity of
KING EDWARD THE SIXTH.

In the front part of the Vestry Minutes commencing (1601) I also find the following, viz.:

> "KING EDWARD THE SIXTH of famous memorie gave unto this parish one annuitie of seaven pounds per annum for ever payable out of his High Court of Exchequer at the feasts of Easter and St. Michaell the Archangell by even portions.

OBSERVATIONS.

There is no date to the above entry, but on going through the old Churchwardens' Accounts, I find in the year 1637, being the first account, and also in the following two years, an entry similar to this, viz.:

> "A Perpetual Annuity
> "Also they charge themselves with the
> "receipt of £VII out of the Exchequer
> "for one year's payment of a pension
> "given to this parish by King Edward
> "the Sixth.

£007 : 00 : 00"

I find no further trace in the accounts of the Gift being received, it thus appears that it was paid for three years, and then stopped; why it was discontinued I have no means of ascertaining.

On searching further through the old Deeds I find the following Grant, viz. :

"8th Nov. 1554 } Philip and Mary by Letters Patent
"1st & 2nd Philip } confirm a Record in the Exchequer
"and Mary } whereby the Barons had allowed a
"Claim made by the Churchwardens of St. Botolph of a
"yearly pension of £7 payable at Easter and Michaelmas
"for the maintenance of the priest there."

This (less the fees payable upon the receipt of the same) is still received by the Vicar, and I am of opinion that it is a confirmation of the 1st *Grant.*

I have made enquiries at the Treasury Offices, but can obtain no information there.

Its value at the date of grant was **£7**, *and presuming that it is the one now received, the value would be the same (less the fees,) at March* 1865.

MRS. ELIZABETH HIBBEN'S GIFT.

Also in front of the old Vestry Minutes, the following entry appears, viz.:

> "ELIZABETH HIBBENS late of London widowe by her last Will and Testament gave to the poore of this parish to be bestowed on a purchase the sum of £100 with which and other monies certain lands and tenements were purchased by this parish in Doelittle Lane and Knight Ryder Street which are of the yearely value of £12 : 6 : 8 per annum whereof is to be distributed at Christmas £5."

OBSERVATIONS.

It does not say in what manner it is to be distributed, nor give the date of the Will, but it must have been prior to 1637, as the Gift is there mentioned, see page 98.

It appears by the Churchwardens' accounts that this was charged upon and distributed out of the rent of the above premises from 1637 to 1649 both inclusive as Mrs Hibben's Gift, but it does not say in what manner. After this time I find no further trace of the Gift as such. See observations on Anderson's and Glassbrooke's Gifts.

These premises, now known as Knight Ryder Court, are still in the possession of the parish, and let to three tenants at the yearly rents of £19, £21, and £12, making together the yearly sum of £52.

The value at the date of bequest was £5 per annum, and being a charge on the above premises, I presume that it would be of the same value at March 1865.

It is not distributed now.

LADY RAMSEY'S GIFT.

Dame Mary Ramsey by Will dated 8th July 1601, bequeathed £2,000 to the Mayor, Commonality, and Citizens of London, to be laid out by the Governors of Christ's Hospital in the purchase of lands, tenements, and hereditaments, of the yearly value of £100, to be assured to the said Mayor, Commonality, and Citizens of London; and out of the rents thereof she directed that £2 yearly should be paid to two preachers, £1 to each, to be appointed by the Treasurer and Governors of Christ's Hospital to preach in Christ's Church yearly two sermons, one on St. Stephen's day, and the other the first Sunday in Lent: and 10s. yearly to the person who should have the keeping of her monument in Christ's Church; and also to the Churchwardens of the said parish, to be disposed according to the necessity of the poor of the said parish, the sum of £2 : 10s. at their discretion, and the remainder of the said yearly value or revenue of £100 to be yearly paid by way of distribution to such and so many of such four parishes in London as to the discretion of the said Govenors should be thought meet, the account thereof to be kept by itself, because the distribution thereof might the better appear.

OBSERVATIONS.

The value of the above Gift at the date of bequest and March 1865 *would appear to be* **£1** *per annum, and every third year we receive the sum of £3 from Christ's Hospital as our portion, but it is entirely at the option of the Governors of the Hospital.*

The last payment of £3 was received in 1868.

It is distributed in money to the poor, the forty prayer people being generally the recipients.

BARNARD HYDE'S GIFT.

By Indenture bearing date 12th December 1630, made between Barnard Hyde of London, Esquire, of the one part, and the Master, Wardens, and Commonality of the Salters' Company of the other part. The said Master, Wardens, and Commonality, in consideration that the said Barnard Hyde had delivered to them certain sums of money, and had given and released to them his share of the lands in the Irish Plantation, covenanted with him that they would within ten years then next purchase lands of the yearly value of £62 at the least, and would bestow the rents thereof as follows : £30 yearly to a godly and learned preacher to be chosen after the decease of the said Barnard Hyde by the said Company, who should be a Master of Arts of five years standing of Cambridge or Oxford, and steadfast in the religion of the Church of England, to preach a lecture or sermon weekly for ever on Tuesday in the afternoon, in the parish Church of St. Dunstan in the East; £5 to be distributed equally amongst ten poor people of the said parish, to be yearly in writing recommended to the said Company by the Parson, Churchwardens, and Overseers of the poor of the same, and in case the said lecture should not be permitted to be continued in the said Church, then the said lecture and lecturer to be tendered to one more or all of the several parishes of St. Mary at Hill, St. Margaret Patten, and Allhallows Barking, London, respectively in the order they stand named, and the said lecture to be there preached till the Parson, and the major part of the parishioners of St. Dunstan should desire that the same should be performed in the Church of that parish which the said Barnard Hyde chiefly desired. And the said £5 per annum before given to the poor of St. Dunstan to be distributed to the poor of the parish where the said lecture should be performed during that time and no longer. And if the said weekly lecture should be by authority suppressed or discontinued so as not to be performed in some one of the parishes before specified, then the said yearly payment of £30 during the time that the said lecture should be discontinued, upon reasonable request, to be paid to the right kin of the said Barnard Hyde; but nevertheless, the said £5 per annum to the poor of St. Dunstan to be yearly paid and continued to them without intermission in manner aforesaid. £5 to be distributed on St. Thomas' Day to ten poor men free of the Salters' Company in such portions as the said Master and Wardens should think fit, having respect to every one's necessity. Twenty shillings to be yearly paid to the Churchwardens of the parish of Little Ilford in Essex upon being demanded at Salters' Hall, to be distributed to such four poor persons dwelling in that parish as they should think most fitting by equal portions. £13 : 10s. to be distributed yearly to fifty-four poor widows or maids of the following parishes, to each 5s. to help to buy them clothes or other necessaries; the distribution thereof to be made the first year in the parishes of St. Dunstan in the East, Allhallows Barking, and St. Botolph without Aldgate, to eighteen poor widows or maids in each of those parishes. The 2nd year in the parishes of St. Mary Whitechapel, St. Botolph Bishopsgate, and St. Leonord Shoreditch. The 3rd year in the parishes of Allhallows in the Wall, St. Stephen Coleman Street, and St. Alphage. The 4th year in the parishes of St. Giles Cripplegate, St. Olave Silver Street, and, instead of a third parish, to eighteen Salters' widows or daughters, such as the Master and Wardens of the said Company should make choice of not being pensioners to the said Company. The 5th year in the parishes of St. Botolph Aldersgate, St. Sepulchre's, and St. Andrew's Holborn. The 6th year in the parishes of St. Bride, St. Anne Blackfriars, and St. Andrew Wardrobe. The 7th year in the parishes of St. Mary Somerset, St. Michael Queenhithe, and All Hallows the Great Thames Street. The 8th year in the parishes of St. Mary Magdalen Bermondsey, St. George's Southwark, and St. Thomas, but not to any pensioners of that Hospital. The 9th year to the parishes of St. Olave Southwark, St. Saviour Southwark, and St. Mary at Hill. The 10th year in the parishes of St. Katherine

Coleman Street, St. Katherine Creechurch, and St. Margaret Pattens; and so every 10th year the distribution to come about again to the same parishes respectively. The said poor widows or maids to be yearly recommended by the Parson, Churchwardens, and Overseers of the several parishes aforesaid, in writing, within three days after notice should be given to them by the beadle of the said Company, which notice the Company agreed should be given ten days before Christmas-day yearly; and the several Churchwardens and Overseers to dispose of the said money in the presence of the Master and Wardens of the said Company. And if there should be any Salters' widows or daughters in any of the same parishes known to the Parson, Churchwardens, and Overseers, or to the said Master, Wardens, or Commonality, to be poor or in want of relief, they were to be preferred before others, as the Master and Wardens should direct. Three pounds to be retained by the Master, Wardens, and officers of the said Company, for their trouble in certain specified shares, and the residue of the profits of the said lands to be yearly disposed of at some loving meeting or otherwise, to the use of the said Company as the said Master and Wardens for the time being should think fitting. And they also covenanted that as to £200 parcel of the said money delivered to them, they would from time to time deliver the same to such four young men, free of the said Company, as would be suitors for the same, upon sufficient security, by £50 a-piece for two years gratis; the same parties not to have the same sum again under two years after the payment of them in respectively.

OBSERVATIONS.

In 1637 £1020 was laid out by the Salters' Company in the purchase of two houses on the west side of Gracechurch Street, and by a declaration of Trust dated 1639 from the trustees to whom these premises were conveyed, they acknowledged that they held them upon the trusts of Barnard Hyde's deed.

The annual sum of £13 : 10s. is distributed amongst fifty-four poor maids and widows of the parishes specified in the above-mentioned Deed in rotation. Notice is given by the beadle of the Company to the three parishes whose turn it is to receive the Gift; a list of eighteen poor maids and widows is sent by the Minister and Churchwardens of each parish, and receipts from them are entered in a book kept by the Clerk of the Company.

The first payment to this parish was due in 1630. There being no Churchwardens' accounts till 1637, I have no information as to its receipt.

It became due again in 1645, but there are no accounts entered for that year.

In 1655, the next time of payment, I find the same received and distributed.

The last receipt of this Gift was in the year 1865.

It is distributed in accordance with the Will.

The value of the Gift at the date of bequest and March 1865 was **9s.** per annum, payable every tenth year, and is duly received from the Salters' Company.

Mr. JOHN CARTER'S GIFT.

John Carter, by his Will bearing date 10th of April, 1780, gave to the Churchwardens of this parish, and their successors, £100 3 per cent Consols, to visit his tombstone in the Church at Edmonton, on the 27th June yearly, and see that the inscription was continued thereon, the dividend to be divided as follows:

	£	s.	d
Coach hire for the Churchwardens	0	6	0
To the Clerk and Sexton of Edmonton	0	4	0
Dinner to the Churchwardens of St. Botolph at Edmonton	1	10	0
To be given in bread on the Sunday after the 27th June yearly, to the poor of the bread list belonging to the parish of St. Botolph	1	0	0
	£3	0	0

OBSERVATIONS.

This Stock now stands in the names of Mr. R. J. Chaplin, Deputy of the Ward, and Mr. John Reynolds.

The amount of the yearly dividends is duly received, out of which 4s. is paid annually to the Clerk and Sexton of Edmonton.

The sum of £1, applicable for the purchase of bread, is distributed by the Churchwardens to the poor at the parish Church on Sundays, and the terms of the Will duly complied with.

Its value at the date of bequest and March 1865 was **£3** *per annum.*

MR. THOMAS TURNER'S GIFT.

Mr. Thomas Turner, by his Will, gave to the Churchwardens of this parish the annual sum of 15s. in consideration of their visiting his tomb at Walthamstowe once a year, and seeing the same is kept in good order.

OBSERVATIONS.

This sum is regularly received by the Churchwardens on their inspection of the tomb.

Its value at the date of bequest, and March 1865, *was* **15s.** *per annum.*

Additional Gift of LADY ANNE PACKINGTON.

This Gift was given by the above lady, and the Clothworkers' Company covenanted with the Dean and Chapter of Westminster to pay the sum of £4 : 13 : 4 yearly, as appears by the following Deed, viz. :

By an Indenture dated 23rd November 1570 the Clothworkers' Company covenanted with the Dean and Chapter of Westminster to pay to the Churchwardens of Saint Botolph Aldersgate for the time being, and to their successors, £4 : 13 : 4 yearly in the Hall of the Company, to the intent that £4 : 6 : 8 part thereof should be by the said Churchwardens and their successors yearly for ever distributed and paid in manner therein mentioned, viz. in payment weekly on every Sunday in the year perpetually to five poor people of the said parish at 4d. each, which would amount to £4 : 6 : 8 per annum, and the residue being 6s. 8d. per annum, the said Churchwardens of the said parish for the time being were to have for their own use, for their pains had and taken in and about the receipt and distribution of the said money so long as they should distribute to the said poor people the said money weekly on every Sunday in manner and form aforesaid.

The Company also thereby further covenanted with the said Dean and Chapter of Westminster, that if the said sum of £4 : 13 : 4 or any part thereof should be unpaid to the said Churchwardens, or their successors, for twenty-eight days after the days of payment therein named being by them or any of them lawfully asked at the said Hall, then and so often the said Company and their successors should pay to the said Dean and Chapter of Westminster, and to the said Churchwardens and their successors for the time being, for every default and by way of penalty 6s. 8d. to be retained by the said Dean and Chapter of Wesminster for their own use in consideration of their pains to be had and taken from time to time in and about the performance of the covenants payments and distributions expressed in the above mentioned Deed. This Deed also contains a proviso covenant and agreement between the said parties thereto (the Company being one of such parties) that in case default shall be made by the said Dean and Chapter of Westminster and the said Churchwardens, or by their successors, in the distribution of the said money in part or in all contrary to the form aforesaid the default proceeding or happening through the wilfulness or negligence of the said Dean and Chapter of Westminster and Churchwardens for the time being or their successors, or any of them, the said yearly payment of £4:13:4 shall cease and no longer be paid to them nor to any of them And from thenceforth the said Company covenanted with the Dean and Chapter of St. Paul and their successors to pay them the said last mentioned sum of £4:13:4 yearly within the Hall of the said Company, to the intent that the Dean &c. of St. Paul and their successors should from thenceforth for ever distribute and pay to five poor people of the said parish of St. Botolph at the times and proportions and in manner aforesaid £4:6:8 yearly, and the residue of the said £4:13:4 viz. 6s. 8d. was to be retained by the said Dean &c. of St. Paul to their own use for their pains to be had and taken in that behalf.

The Deed also contains a stipulation for payment by the Company to the Dean &c. of St. Paul of 6s. 8d. for every default in payment by them of the said sum of £4:13:4 at the time and place before mentioned to be retained by the said Dean and Chapter of St. Paul for their own use for their pains in and about the receiving and distribution of the said money. The Deed further contains a covenant to pay the sum of 6s. 8d. yearly to the Dean and Chapter of St. Paul for their pains in seeing to the due execution of the trust.

This Gift was not received after Michaelmas 1827, *but in* 1866 *the matter was brought under the consideration of the Charity Commissioners, and a scheme was suggested, when, after due notice being given on the Church, the following Order was made:*

"CHARITY COMMISSION.

"In the matter of Dame Anne Packington's Charity in the Parish of St. Botolph without Aldersgate in the the City of London.

"The Board of Charity Commissioners for England and Wales having considered an application in writing made to them on the twelfth day of March One thousand eight hundred and sixty-six in the matter of the above mentioned Charity for the purposes of the following order. And it appearing to the said Board that the endowment of the said Charity consists of the particulars mentioned in the Schedule hereto, and that the gross annual income of the said Charity amounts to Nine pounds eight shillings, and that there are not any legally constituted Trustees of the said Charity. And that it is for the advantage of the said Charity that such Trustees should be appointed, and that a scheme should be established for the future regulation of the said Charity. And upon notice of the intention of the said Board to make the Order hereinafter contained having been given by the affixing of the same according to the direction of the said Board to the principal outer door of the Parish Church of Saint Botolph Without Aldersgate aforesaid, on the tenth day of May One thousand eight hundred and sixty-six, being more than one calendar month previously to the date hereof, and no notice of any sufficient objection to the said proposed Order or suggestion for the variation thereof having been received by the said Board. Do hereby order that the Incumbent and Churchwardens of the aforesaid Parish of Saint Botolph Without Aldersgate, and their respective successors for the time being, in right and during tenure of their said respective offices be appointed to be the Trustees for the administration of the said Charity.

"And the said Board do further order, by way of scheme for the future regulation of the said Charity, that the clear annual income thereof which shall remain after the payment thereout of the yearly sum of Six shillings and eightpence to the Dean and Chapter of the

Cathedral Church of Saint Paul's London, in pursuance of the terms of the foundation of the Charity, shall be applied to the benefit of the most deserving and necessitous inhabitants of the aforesaid Parish of Saint Botolph Without Aldersgate to be selected for this purpose by the said Trustees, by providing them with clothes, bedding, fuel, medical or other aid in sickness, food or other articles in kind, or with pecuniary aid in special cases, as shall be considered by the Trustees to be most advantageous to them, and that either directly, or by aiding the funds of any provident or friendly Associations to which they shall belong, or any public Institutions of which respectively it shall be the object to provide them with like benefits, and so that no funds of the Charity shall be applied directly or indirectly to the relief of the poor rates of the said Parish."

SCHEDULE REFERRED TO IN THE ABOVE ORDER.

The sum of £313 : 6 : 8 Consolidated £3 per cent. Annuities, which is held by "The Official Trustees of Charitable Funds" in trust for the said Charity.

Sealed by order of the Board this thirteenth day of November One thousand eight hundred and sixty-six.

HENRY W. VANE, Secretary.

The statement sent by the Clothworkers' Company to the Charity Commissioners is as follows, viz.:

Amount of arrears on account of the sums annually payable according to the terms of the before-mentioned Indenture dated 23rd November, 1570, and the Will of the Dame Ann Packington, viz. :

Arrears of the sum of £4 : 13 : 4 payable annually to the Churchwardens of St. Botolph (for distribution : 20d. every Sunday weekly to five poor people of St. Botolph, 4d. each, and 6s. 8d. yearly to the Churchwardens for their pains in receipt and

distribution) from 29th September, 1827, to 29th September, 1865	£177	6	8
Additional amount payable 29th September, 1866 ..	4	13	4
	£182	0	0
Arrears of the sum of 6s. 8d. payable annually to the Dean and Chapter of St. Paul's from 29th September, 1856 (date of the last payment)	3	0	0
Additional amount payable 29th September, 1866 ..	0	6	8
	£185	6	8
Original Endowment..............	100	0	0
	£285	6	8

OBSERVATIONS.

The sum of £313 : 6 : 8 *now stands in the* £3 *per cent annuities in the names of the Charity Commissioners, and the Dividend is payable to and received by the Churchwardens, and distributed in conformity with the above Order.*

The value at the date of bequest was £4 : 13 : 4 *per annum, and at the present time it is* **£9 : 8s.** *per annum.*

The value at March 1865 was uncertain.

MR. H. O. CURETON'S GIFT.

Mr. HARRY OSBORN CURETON, by his Will dated 19th July 1858, gave as follows:—

"I give to the Minister, Churchwardens, and Overseers of the "parish of St. Botolph, Aldersgate, in the City of London, for "the time being, the sum of £2000 Three per cent. Consols to "be placed in the Government Stock or Stocks, and it is my will, "that the interest shall be applied to the purchase of coals every "winter, to be given to poor housekeepers, and also to lodgers; "but in each case they must have lived for two years in this "parish at the least before they apply for the same, and they "must be of sober and good habits. It is, however, my wish, that "out of the interest the minister shall have the sum of 40s. for his "trouble in making it known in the church, two or three Sundays "before the coals are delivered, so that proper persons may apply, "and that the Churchwardens and the Overseers, for the time "being, shall have the sum of £5 out of the said interest, for their "trouble in seeing to the proper distribution of my gift."

OBSERVATIONS.

£200 Consols, part of the above mentioned legacy, was paid for legacy duty, leaving the sum of **£1800**, which is invested as directed by the Will and the Dividends regularly received.

The above gift is annually distributed among the poor of the parish in coals in accordance with the Will of the donor.

PARISH ESTATES.

A

A RETURN

OF

PARISH ESTATES,

HOW ACQUIRED,

AND

THEIR ANNUAL VALUES

AT THE

DATES OF ACQUISITION AND MARCH 1865,

AND

HOW EACH HAVE BEEN APPROPRIATED.

COPY PRESENT TRUST DEED.

THIS INDENTURE made the 17th day of November 1865 between GEORGE MILLS of No. 15 Goswell Street and formerly of Long Lane in the parish of Saint Botolph Without Aldersgate in the City of London coach maker of the first part ROBERT BESLEY of Fann Street in the said parish one of the aldermen of the said City of London JOHN SEWELL of No. 65 Aldersgate Street in the same parish builder ROBERT JAMES CHAPLIN of No. 25 Aldersgate Street aforesaid gentleman CHARLES MANN of No. 159 Aldersgate Street aforesaid butcher EDWARD LANE of No. 6 Aldersgate Street aforesaid straw hat manufacturer WILLIAM MASTERS of No. 13 Aldersgate Street aforesaid brush maker JOHN ELDER DUFFIELD of No. 3 Long Lane in the said parish coach builder and harness maker JOHN HERRING of No. 40 Aldersgate Street aforesaid wholesale druggist GEORGE SIMS of No. 150 Aldersgate Street aforesaid looking-glass manufacturer HENRY PIPER of No. 21 Aldersgate Street aforesaid gentleman WILLIAM WALLFORD of No. 159 Aldersgate Street aforesaid surgeon THOMAS BLAKE of 129 Aldersgate Street aforesaid wholesale clothier THOMAS ILLMAN of No. 20 Little Britain in the said parish packing case maker CHARLES JAMES ELLETT of No. 8 Jewin Street in the said parish cabinet maker THOMAS HENRY ELLIS of No, 51 Jewin Street aforesaid engraver JAMES BOOTE GOODINGE of No. 21 Aldersgate Street aforesaid stationer EDMUND FOX of No. 75A Little Britain aforesaid photograph mounter and THOMAS BLYVERS FLOYD of No. 36 Aldersgate Street aforesaid gentleman of the second part and HENRY DE JERSEY of No. 13 Gresham Street West in the said City of London gentleman of the third part WHEREAS by Indenture of lease and re-lease, the re-lease dated the 20th day of January 1824 and made between John Ramsbottom John Reid Grantham Mead Thomas Loveland Joseph Turner John Lorkin and Joseph Fothergill (therein described as the surviving trustees of the messuages lands tenements and hereditaments hereinafter described and intended to be hereby granted) of the one part and Benjamin Fuller

Hopkins Thomas Lister Forrest William Walton Thomas Lloyd John Smith Thomas Summers Robert Biggar William Lewis Nicholl Francis Henry Groom John Collender the said George Mills James Whitbourn and Thrower Herring of the other part All and singular the said messuages lands tenements and hereditaments hereinafter described and intended to be hereby conveyed with the appurtenances were re-leased and conveyed to the use of the said Benjamin Fuller Hopkins Thomas Lister Forrest William Walton Thomas Lloyd John Smith Thomas Summers Robert Biggar William Lewis Nicholl Francis Henry Groom John Collander George Mills James Whitbourn Thrower Herring John Ramsbottom John Reid Grantham Mead Thomas Loveland Joseph Turner John Lorkin and Joseph Fothergill their heirs and assigns for ever upon the trust thereinafter expressed and declared concerning the said hereditaments being trusts in all respects similar to the trusts hereinafter declared concerning the same hereditaments AND WHEREAS the said Benjamin Fuller Hopkins Thomas Lister Forrest William Walton John Smith Thomas Sumners Robert Biggar William Lewis Nicholl Francis Henry Groom John Collander James Whitbourn Thrower Herring John Ramsbottom John Reid Grantham Mead Thomas Loveland Joseph Turner and Joseph Fothergill have all departed this life AND WHEREAS by an Indenture dated the 8th day of November 1838 and expressed to be made between the said Thomas Lloyd of the first part and the said Benjamin Fuller Hopkins Thomas Lister Forrest Thomas Summers Robert Biggar William Lewis Nicholl Francis Henry Groom John Collander George Mills James Whitbourn (therein called Whitbourne) Thrower Herring Grantham Mead Joseph Robert Biggar John Lorkin and Joseph Fothergill of the second part the said Thomas Lloyd did hereby demise re-lease and quit claim unto the parties thereto of the second part their heirs and assigns all the estate right title share or shares interest use trust claim and demand whatsoever of him the said Thomas Lloyd to or out of the said hereditaments hereinafter described and intended to be hereby conveyed to the intent that the said parties thereto of the second part their heirs and assigns might henceforth stand seized of the same hereditaments upon the trusts declared concerning the same by the hereinbefore recited Indenture of the 20th day of January 1824

AND WHEREAS the said John Lorkin and George Mills were at the time of the holding of the general vestry next hereinafter mentioned the sole surviving or continuing trustees of the said hereditaments hereinafter described and intended to be hereby conveyed AND WHEREAS at a general vestry of the parish of Saint Botolph Without Aldersgate holden on Thursday the 11th day of August 1864 and at another general vestry of the same parish held on Thursday the 13th day of March now last it having been stated that the said John Lorkin and George Mills were the only surviving or continuing trustees under the thereinbefore recited Indenture resolutions were moved and seconded and carried unanimously that the said Robert Besley John Sewell Robert James Chaplin Charles Mann Edward Lane William Masters John Elder Duffield John Herring George Sims Henry Piper William Wallford Thomas Blake Thomas Illman Charles James Ellett Thomas Henry Ellis James Boote Godinge Edmund Fox and Thomas Blyvers Floyd should be and be appointed new trustees jointly with the said surviving and continuing trustees of the said messuages lands tenements and hereditaments hereinafter described and intended to be hereby conveyed for and on behalf of the said parish of Saint Botolph Without Aldersgate and that a new deed of trust should be prepared and that the said John Lorkin and George Mills should convey the same hereditaments to such new trustees and upon the trusts hereinafter appearing AND WHEREAS the said John Lorkin died on the fifth day of November 1865 NOW THIS INDENTURE WITNESSETH that in pursuance of the said agreement and for effectuating the said resolutions of the said general vestry and in consideration of the premises he the said George Mills as such sole surviving and continuing trustee as aforesaid doth hereby grant and confirm unto the said Henry De Jersey his heirs and assigns all and singular the messuages lands tenements and hereditaments which are mentioned enumerated or described in the schedule hereunder written and every part and parcel of the same with their and every of their rights members easements and appurtenances and all the estate right title interest claim and demand whatsoever of the said George Mills into and upon the same hereditaments to have and to hold the said hereditaments and all and singular other the premises hereinbefore expressed to be hereby granted unto the said Henry De Jersey his heirs and assigns to the use of the said George Mills Robert Besley John Sewell Robert James Chaplin Charles Mann Edward Lane William Masters John Elder Duffield John Herring George Sims Henry Piper William Wallford Thomas Blake Thomas Illman Charles James Ellett Thomas Henry Ellis James Boote Goodinge Edmund Fox and Thomas Blyvers Floyd their heirs and assigns for ever Upon trust and confidence nevertheless and to the intent that they the said George Mills Robert Besley John Sewell Robert James Chaplin Charles Mann Edward Lane William Masters John Elder Duffield John Herring George Sims Henry Piper William Wallford Thomas Blake Thomas Illman Charles James Ellett Thomas Henry Ellis James Boote Goodinge Edmund Fox and Thomas Blyvers Floyd and the survivors and survivor of them and the heirs of such survivor their and his assigns shall at all times hereafter convey demise lease and dispose of the said hereditaments and premises to such person and persons and in such manner and form as the parishioners of the said parish of Saint Botolph Without Aldersgate assembled in vestry in order to treat and order the business and affairs of the said parish shall from time to time order direct and appoint and shall do and for ever hereafter permit and suffer the churchwardens for the time being of the goods chattels rents and ornaments of the church of the said parish of Saint Botolph Without Aldersgate from time to time and at all times hereafter to receive and take the rents issues and profits of the same hereditaments and premises as the same shall from time to time arise grow due and be payable as formerly hath been used and for such charitable uses intents and purposes as the same have been usually disposed of and employed by the parishioners of the said parish whether in or about the repairs of the said church the relief of the poor of the same parish or any other the public affairs of the same parish and to and for no other use trust or purpose whatever And the said George Mills doth hereby for himself his heirs executors and administrators covenant with the said Henry De Jersey his heirs and assigns that the said George Mills hath not heretofore done or willingly permitted or suffered anything whereby or by reason whereof the hereditaments and premises hereinbefore expressed to be hereby granted or any of them or any part thereof are is or may be impeached effected or encumbered in title estate or otherwise IN

WITNESS whereof the said parties to these presents have hereunto set their hands and seals the day and year first above written.

THE SCHEDULE HEREINBEFORE REFERRED TO.

FIRST—All that messuage or tenement with the warehouse buildings and appurtenances to the same belonging known as No. 129 Aldersgate Street in the said parish of Saint Botolph Without Aldersgate in the City of London and let on lease for a term of years to Haven Kaye and in the occupation of his undertenants or assigns And also all that messuage or tenement with the buildings and appurtenances to the same belonging known as No. 128 Aldersgate Street aforesaid whereof a portion on the north side abuts on Now Street Cloth Fair in the parish of Saint Bartholomew the Great West Smithfield in the City of London all which last-mentioned premises are now in the occupation of John Thomas Norris as lessee or his undertenants or assigns and the said premises first hereinbefore described were heretofore known by the description following (that is to say) all that brick messuage or tenement and the warehouses behind the same erected and built in and upon a certain piece or parcel of ground lying and being in Aldersgate Street in the said parish of Saint Botolph Without Aldersgate near the Peacock formerly there containing in front towards Aldersgate Street aforesaid (including the way or passage leading out of Aldersgate Street to two brick messuages heretofore on lease to Captain William Smith and afterwards partly in the occupation of John Middleton and the remainder whereon part of the workhouse stood in the tenure of Rebecca Leader chymist) twelve yards one foot and one inch or thereabouts and the whole piece of ground in length from Aldersgate Street aforesaid extending westward ninety-nine feet and one half or thereabouts on the west side thereof and on other ground being the inheritance of the said parishioners and purchased by them of William Denton and others were standing the said two messuages or tenements belonging to the said Captain William Smith and let to him from the trustees of the said parish at fifteen pounds a-year rent and which was formerly the garden of the prior and convent of Saint Bartholomew and on which said piece or parcel of ground lately stood a tenement with sollars and cellars called the

Church House and was formerly divided into several tenements and theretofore in the several tenures or occupations of Stephen Taylor baker Simon Newbolt victualler Elizabeth Stevens widow and John Holland innholder and formerly described and known by the name of all that messuage or tenement fronting Aldersgate Street on the west side of the same street and all that messuage or building containing several rooms lying backwards of the said front messuage all along on the south side of the courtyard or passage leading out of Aldersgate Street to the said two messuages or tenements of Captain William Smith and which said messuages or tenements and rooms were since in lease to Henry Jessop baker from the said parish at the yearly rent of twenty-five pounds and were in the tenure or occupation of the said Henry Jessop baker his undertenants or assigns and also by the name of all that other front messuage fronting Aldersgate Street aforesaid on the west side of the said street and situate standing and being on the south side of the said passage leading out of Aldersgate Street aforesaid to the said two brick messuages or tenements on lease to the said Captain William Smith as aforesaid and which said messuage was heretofore in the tenure or occupation of   and since of
                    and then called or known by the name or sign of The Crooked Billet and used as a publichouse and was on lease to George Gregory deceased and in the tenure or occupation of Robert Crow wire drawer and which said brick messuage and warehouses behind the same and then let by the said parish of Saint Botolph Without Aldersgate unto Edward Parker for the term of thirty years and afterwards in the tenure or occupation of Messieurs Hall and Brooks and then in the tenure or occupation of the British Assurance Society on a lease at seventy pounds per annum

SECONDLY—And also all that other messuage or tenement with the garden and appurtenances thereto belonging situate in Aldersgate Street aforesaid within the said parish of Saint Botolph Without Aldersgate now known as No. 164 Aldersgate Street aforesaid and in the occupation of George Ellwood his undertenants or assigns which said messuage or tenement was formerly divided and converted into three tenements and in the tenure or occupation of Thomas Weary Esquire and John Shallcross schoolmaster their undertenants or assigns and was afterwards described and known as follows videlicit All that messuage or tenement fronting Aldersgate Street on the west side of the said street with a little garden behind the same and also that small tenement lying behind the same situate on the south side of the entry or passage leading out of Aldersgate Street into another brick messuage or tenement heretofore used as a tavern by Joseph Haywood and since in the tenure or occupation of Roger Griffin his undertenants or assigns and also all that other brick messuage or tenement lying backwards of the said two messuages or tenements and heretofore used as a tavern as aforesaid and which contained the admeasurements hereinafter mentioned that is to say from the street towards the west on the north side one hundred and thirty-one and a half feet or thereabouts and from the street towards the west on the south side one hundred and twenty-six feet little more or less and in front towards the street from north to south thirty-one feet four inches and from north to south in the rear at the west including a slip of ground let by lease to Mr. Normansell thirty-two feet six inches all which said last-mentioned premises were heretofore on lease from the said parish to Gilbert Morrison at the yearly rent of ten pounds clear of all taxes and were lately in the tenure or occupation of Thomas Denham and William Shaw and late were leased or agreed to be leased to William Hodgson for forty years and were then in the possession or occupation of Mr. Hugh Bell

THIRDLY—And also all that other messuage or tenement situate in Aldersgate Street aforesaid and now known as No. 165 in the same street and let on lease for a term of years to and late in the occupation of the trustees of the City of London Literary and Scientific Institution and now in the occupation of the Young Men's Christian Association and which said premises were formerly known by the description following (that is to say) all that long slip piece or parcel of ground which was heretofore taken out of and was part of the garden formerly belonging to one John Shallcross schoolmaster and contained in length from east to west on the south side thereof forty-two feet of assize (little more or less) and in breadth from north to south on the east side thereof three feet five inches of assize (little more or less) on which said slip piece or parcel of ground stood the north wall of a house built by Richard Normansell gentleman deceased

FOURTHLY—And also all that messuage or tenement situate and being No. 166 in Aldersgate Street aforesaid known as the Old Parr's Head public-house and let on lease for a term of years to and late in the occupation of Thomas Jones and now in the occupation of Jeremiah Gough And also all that messuage or tenement situate and being No. 167 in Aldersgate Street aforesaid let on lease for a term of years to James Ward and now in the occupation of Nettleship the sites or ground plots of which said premises fourthly hereinbefore described were formerly known by the description following (that is to say) All that piece or parcel of ground (part whereof was formerly an entry) heretofore in the occupation of the said Richard Normansell and since of Zachariah Foxall Esquire deceased and was formerly taken out of the kitchen belonging to Trinity Hall on the other part thereof was also taken out of the said kitchen on the south-east part of which said piece or parcel of ground the said Richard Normansell built a messuage or tenement which said piece or parcel of ground contained in length from east to west on the north side thereof nineteen feet (more or less) and from north to south on the west side thereof seventeen feet (more or less) and from west to east on the south side thereof ten feet more or less and extended from north to south in a straight line on the east side thereof and contained   feet (more or less) and then extended from east to west on the south side thereof and contained nine feet (more or less) and then extended further from south to north on the east side thereof and contained   feet (more or less) which said two pieces or parcels of ground and premises were situate in and near Aldersgate Street in the parish of Saint Botolph Without Aldersgate aforesaid and were in the tenure or occupation of Messrs. Dickinson and Bloxam All which premises thirdly and fourthly hereinbefore described were formerally known and conveyed by the ancient description following (that is to say) " All that messuage or tene-
" ment called Trinity Hall otherwise the Common Hall of the
" Fraternity or Guilds of the Holy Trinity founded in the parish
" church of Saint Botolph Without Aldersgate London aforesaid and
" now dissolved and the kitchen and buttery of the same belonging
" and appertaining and now or heretofore used therewith and also
" All that room now or late used for a kitchen near to the said Hall

" containing in length from north to south fifteen feet of assize
" (little more or less) and in breadth from east to west ten feet of
" assize (little more or less) and one parlour on the east side of the
" same kitchen on the same floor containing in length from north to
" south sixteen feet four inches of assize (little more or less) and in
" breadth from east to west fifteen feet of assize (little more or less)
" lying and being under Trinity Hall aforesaid And also one cellar
" under the said parlour containing in length from north to south
" fourteen feet of assize (little more or less) and from east to
" west twelve feet of assize (little more or less) and one yard paved
" with freestone containing from north to south eleven feet four
" inches of assize and from east to west eight feet of assize (little
" more or less) Together with all ways and passages out of the
" said court into and from the said premises and every part thereof
" with all other ways passages staircases cellars and easements
" into and from the said Hall or any room or rooms belonging to
" the same with their and every of their appurtenances All which
" said last-mentioned hereditaments and premises are situate lying
" and being in Aldersgate Street and Trinity Court aforesaid in the
" parish aforesaid and were formerly in the several tenures or occupa-
" tions of John Silk and Samuel Walker their undertenants or
" assigns And also all that messuage or tenement situate and
" standing on the north-west side of Aldersgate Street under and
" near Trinity Hall in the said parish of Saint Botolph heretofore in
" the tenure or occupation of John Silk part of which said premises
" were purchased by the said parish of Saint Botolph Aldersgate
" of the Mayor Commonality and Citizens of the City of London
" Governors of the possessions revenues and goods of the hospitals
" of Edward King of England the sixth of Christ Bridewell and Saint
" Thomas the Apostle as Governors of Christ's Hospital And also
" those two rooms adjoining to Trinity Hall formerly purchased of
"   by the said parish of Saint Botolph
" Aldersgate but now or late of Richard Ward on lease at the
" yearly rent of fifty pounds." And also (by way of conveyance)
All and singular other the hereditaments and premises (if any) not
comprised in the parcels thirdly and fourthly hereinbefore described
which now represent or form part of the said messuage or tenement
called Trinity Hall and other the premises lastly hereinbefore

described or any of them respectively or any part thereof

FIFTHLY—And also all that other messuage or tenement with the appurtenances situate lying and being within the same parish of Saint Botolph Without Aldersgate in the churchyard of the said parish church aforesaid formerly in the tenure or occupation of Simon Kingsland afterwards of Doctor Wells Thomas Hoskins and Doctor Moore afterwards of   and formerly on lease to Robert James for twenty-one years and then on lease to the trustees of Aldersgate Ward Charity School and now let on lease for a term of years to William Cave Fowler and in the occupation of him or his undertenants or assigns

SIXTHLY—And also all that other small messuage or tenement and premises formerly in the occupation of Daniel Adcock situate and being in the south corner of a passage leading into the churchyard belonging to the said parish now known as No. 77 Little Britain and now let on lease for a term of years to the said William Cave Fowler and in the occupasion of him or his undertenants or assigns

SEVENTHLY—And also all those five other messuages or tenements formerly one tenement and now distinguished by the Nos. 4 5 6 7 and 8 in Maidenhead Court in the said parish respectively in the occupation of John Reynolds Ann Glover William Welch and John Aitchison their respective undertenants or assigns and which said premises were heretofore known by the description following (that is to say) And also all that other tenement or building erected and built upon a certain piece of land with the appurtenances situate in the said parish of Saint Botolph Without Aldersgate London in a certain alley called Lamb Alley otherwise Maidenhead Alley in Maidenhead Court for some time past used with other premises thereto adjoining as a workhouse for the poor of the said parish and which said piece or parcel of ground and buildings thereon were formerly in the tenure or occupation of William Plumstead and also of   Porter his undertenants or assigns and were formerly described and known by the names of All those three messuages or tenements in Maidenhead Court aforesaid divided and let out into several tenements by James Rhodes deceased and whose widow held the same from the said parishioners of Saint

Botolph Without Aldersgate at the yearly rent of ten pounds and which said premises were afterwards by virtue of an Indenture of lease granted to one James Barreyman at the yearly rent of thirty pounds

EIGHTHLY—And also all that other messuage or tenement situate and being No. 141 in Aldersgate Street aforesaid and two other messuages and dwelling-houses in the rear thereof situate in a court there formerly called Black Horse Alley now part of and entered from Bowman's Buildings in the said parish as the same three messuages were formerly in the occupation of Thomas Lloyd and now or late let on lease for a term of years to John Hare and in the occupation of him or his undertenants or assigns And also all that other messuage or tenement situate and being No. 140 in Aldersgate Street aforesaid in the occupation of William Wray Cork his undertenants or assigns All which four messuages were heretofore known by the description following (that is to say) All that other capital messuage heretofore called The Black Horse and all other houses messuages and tenements thereto belonging as the same were situate and being in an alley called Black Horse Alley otherwise Little Horse Alley within the said parish of Saint Botolph Without Aldersgate London aforesaid with all the profits commodities and appurtenances to the same belonging or appertaining heretofore pulled down and built into four messuages or tenements and then described and known as followeth (that is to say) All those two messuages or tenements fronting Aldersgate Street situate on the west side of the same street with yards to the same And also all those two other messuages or tenements situate and lying directly behind the same with a garden and yard to each and all which four messuages or tenements yards and gardens were formerly on lease from the said parish to Thomas Turner deceased one of which said front houses was on lease to Walter Crow at twenty-five pounds a-year afterwards in the possession of William Walton since of   and now or late of Timothy Lane another of which front houses was formerly on lease to Charles Kemp since in the possession of Jonathan Jiles and then of Philip Payne and one of which said back houses was formerly in the possession of Robert Witham at ten pounds a-year and then of   Mitton widow and the other of which said back houses was formerly in the possession of

Thomas Slater at nine pounds a-year and after that in the occupation of   Mitton widow and then of the said Philip Payne and which said four houses contained the admeasurements following (that is to say) in the front from north to south forty-three feet three inches (little more or less) and in depth from east to west on the south side eighty-eight feet four inches and in depth from east to west on the north side 106 feet 4 inches (little more or less) and in breadth at the west and from north to south thirty-three feet three inches (little more or less).

NINTHLY—And also all that messuage or tenement with the garden thereto belonging situate and being No. 142 in Aldersgate Street aforesaid let on lease for a term of years to Richard Rayner and in the occupation of him or his undertenants or assigns and which said messuage and premises were formerly known by the description following (that is to say) All that messuage or tenement and All that garden to the same belonging situate in the parish of Saint Botolph Without Aldersgate in the same street called Aldersgate Street between the tenement and garden formerly in the tenure or occupation of Julian Robinson since of
Chetwin widow and then of
on the south part of the said messuage or tenement then called Black Horse Alley on the north part and the tenement theretofore of Robert Burgoine towards the west and the said street called Aldersgate Street on the east part thereof and formerly in the tenure or occupation of William Butler since of
                     and then of   and formerly described and known as followeth (that is to say) All that messuage or tenement fronting Aldersgate Street and situate on the west side of the same street in the said parish of Saint Botolph Without Aldersgate London together with the yard and garden lying behind the same abutting north upon the messuages or tenements called Black Horse Alley south on a messuage or tenement formerly in the occupation of   since of
                          and then of James Slatford and east on the said street called Aldersgate street All which last-mentioned messuage yard garden and premises were heretofore on lease from the said parish to Walter Langford deceased afterwards in the tenure or occupation of Ann Spane since of Michael

Barlow and then of Paul Postan and contained the admeasurements following (that is to say) in the front from north to south twenty feet and from east to west on the north side eighty-eight feet (or thereabouts) and from east to west on the south side eighty-one feet four inches and from north to south on the west end twenty feet six inches (or thereabouts) all which said premises hereinbefore mentioned were some time part of the possessions of our late Sovereign Lord King James the First in right of His Highnesse's Crown of England

TENTHLY—And also All that messuage or tenement with the appurtenances situate and being on the west side of and being No. 5 Little Knight Rider Court formerly called Dolittle Lane in the parish of Saint Mary Magdalen Old Fish Street in the City of London let on lease for a term of years to Charles Godwin and now in the occupation of him or his undertenants or assigns and containing in length in front next the said lane sixteen feet six inches of assize (or thereabouts) and in depth at the south side nine feet three inches (or thereabouts) and in depth on the north side ten feet three inches (or thereabouts) and in length on the west side sixteen feet (or thereabouts)

ELEVENTHLY—And also all the warehouse and stable situate in Knight Rider Court Old Fish Street in the City of London and now in the occupation of   Bellamy his undertenants or assigns And all that messuage or tenement lying on the north side of and adjoining the said warehouse and stable in Knight Rider Court aforesaid late on lease to William Philp and in the occupation of him or his undertenants or assigns with their respective appurtenances all which said warehouse stable and messuage were formerly known by the description following (that is to say) All that other brick building adjoining on the north to the said hereinbefore mentioned messuage or tenement and premises consisting of a warehouse and stable containing in front next the said lane thirty-two feet two inches (or thereabouts) and in depth on the north side twenty-six feet three inches (or thereabouts) and in depth on the south side twenty-seven feet (or thereabouts) and in length on the west side thirty-one feet two inches (or thereabouts) all which said hereditaments and premises abut east on Dolittle Lane aforesaid west on a messuage belonging to the Worshipful Company of Embroiderers and on certain premises in Knowles Court now or late in the tenure of   south on a messuage belonging to the said company and north on premises in the said court in the tenure of   and the same were formerly in the tenure or occupation of Sir Robert Ladbroke his undertenants or assigns And also the yards behind the same and all other the appurtenances thereto belonging or appertaining Together also with the ground and soil of all and singular the said premises hereby re-leased or intended so to be and on which said ground and soil formerly stood three old brick messuages or tenements which were by Indenture of lease bearing date on or about the 3rd day of April in the year of Our Lord 1765 granted and demised by William Tyser Robert Walsham and Andrew Jordaine John Brindley John Sharp Richard Panton and Henry Walker James Tomlinson and John Ford then surviving feoffees or trustees for the said parish of Saint Botolph Without Aldersgate and William Riddlesdon and John Bywater the then churchwardens of the said parish to Sir Robert Ladbroke Knight since deceased for sixty-one years from Lady Day then next at the yearly rent of ten pounds payable quarterly clear of all taxes and deductions whatsoever which said old messuages and premises the said Sir Robert Ladbroke was by the said lease at liberty to pull down and to erect a stable or stabling or other building or buildings upon the said premises so demised to him as aforesaid or some part thereof as he should think proper of as great or greater value by the year as the premises thereby demised and which the said Sir Robert Ladbroke accordingly did

Duly signed by all parties and attested

A piece of ground in the Cloath Fair of Great St. Bartholomew near West Smithfield
FREEHOLD

17th October 1657.

EDWARD DENTON by his Will devises all his houses with the appurtenances (int alia) in or near Aldersgate Street wherein he had any estate of inheritance or other estates unto his uncles William Denton and Edward Furst and his brother Alexander Denton and their heirs for ever Upon trust that the same should be sold by them or the survivors or survivor of them or the heirs of such survivor for the best price that could be got for the same and the money to be applied for the payment of his debts

30th April 1658.

BY FEOFFMENT (inrolled in Chancery 23rd July 1658) Reciting the Will of Edmund Denton the said William Denton Edward Furst and Alexander Denton in consideration of £140 did by the order and appointment of the parishioners of the said parish of St. Botolph grant &c.

"All that piece and parcel of waste ground lying and being within the Cloath Fair of Great St. Bartholomew near West Smithfield London with four booths thereon standing in the east end of the said Cloath Fair abutting on the stone wall there on the east and the garden of Sir John Brockett knight on the south and the booths and waste ground demised to Bartholomew Betts on the north and openeth upon the Cloath Fair aforesaid on the west and also that part of the stone wall except such and so much as others have already builded upon and the part of the brick wall and the ground and soil whereupon those parts of the said stone wall and brick wall do stand adjoining upon the said waste ground and containing in length from the waste ground demised to the said Bartholomew Betts along by the said stone wall towards the garden of the said John Brockett aforesaid twenty-two feet besides the thickness of the brick wall and from the outside of the said stone wall along by the said brick wall towards the Cloath Fair nineteen feet besides the thickness of the said stone wall and from the said stone wall along by the said waste ground demised to the said Bartholomew Betts towards the Cloath Fair twenty-six feet besides the thickness of the said stone wall and from the said waste ground demised to the said Bartholomew Betts along by the Cloth Fair to the said brick wall thirty feet besides the thickness of the said brick wall Upon which said piece of waste ground there is now erected and built a new stable And also all that waste ground between the said erected and new built stable and the tenement and backside there belonging to Thomas Swynowe and now in the occupation of John Ellyard which said waste ground was left to the said Sir Henry Marten when the said tenement was lately erected and new built by the said Thomas Swynowe for the necessary passage of him his horses and coach from and to the said stable the breadth thereof contains thirteen feet five inches (or thereabouts) and the length thereof from the new coach-house door to the garden wall thirty-one feet (or thereabouts) All the said premises in the tenure of the said Sir Henry Marten Unto James Fletcher and twenty-five others their heirs and assigns for ever Upon trust that the rents of the said premises be applied to and for the performance of charitable uses as is appointed by the last Will of Christopher Tamworth Esquire dated 28th April 1624 the money with which the same was purchased being raised by the the sale of a farm and lands in or near Vang in Essex formerly purchased by the money of the said Christopher Tamworth for charitable uses"

A Leasehold Estate in Petty Wales, in the Parish of Great St. Bartholomew, West Smithfield, London, under Lease from the Warden and Scholars of St. Mary College, of Winchester and Oxford, commonly called New College, in Oxford.

19th July, 1638. *14th Charles.*

THE warden and scholars of the New College, by lease for the considerations therein mentioned, did demise, grant, and to farm, let unto Sir Henry Marten

"All those their nine messuages cottages or tenements of late in the several tenures or occupations of Richard Lambe, John Strange, John Engarsby, Hugh Parson, John Sterne, John Hower, John Cockle, Agnes Roberts, and Henry Johnson and then in the several tenures or occupations of the said Sir Henry Marten and Richard Tyrrell or one of them Together with the yards gardens and buildings then newly erected and built by the said Sir Henry Marten with all entries ways sollars cellars grounds profits commodities emoluments and other hereditaments whatsoever then in the several tenures or occupations of the said Sir Henry Marten, Ralph Keble or any of them in anywise belonging or appertaining situate lying and being in Petty Wales or elsewhere in the parish of Great St. Bartholomew nigh West Smithfield London with frank and free ingress egress and regress unto and from the said garden messuages buildings cottages or tenements and every of them with their appurtenances at all time and times to and for the said Henry Marten his executors administrators and assigns in by and through the entrys and ways thereunto then used and accustomed"

To hold unto the said Sir Henry Marten his executors administrators and assigns, from Lady-day then last past, for the term of 40 years

At the yearly rent of £8, payable half-yearly.

With power of re-entry in case the rent should not be paid for thirty days after such half-yearly day of payment.

Covenant from Sir Henry Marten to repair the said premises, and keep the same in repair.

Proviso That the said lease should not be assigned without a special license from the said college in writing.

Covenant for quiet possession.

Same date.

The said college granted a special license in writing to the said Sir Henry Marten to assign the said lease.

23rd August, 1641.

Sir Henry Marten made his Will, and appointed Henry Marten his son sole executor thereof, who proved the same in the Prerogative Court of Canterbury on the 15th October following.

12th August, 1642.

By assignment between the said Henry Marten of the one part, and Dame Mary Rogers widow of the other part

Reciting lease from the Dean and Chapter of the College of St. Peter, Westminster, parson of the parish of St. Botolph, and the wardens and parishioners of the said parish, to Sir Henry Marten deceased (dated 18th December, 2nd Charles) of the church-house for sixty years at the yearly rent of 33s. 4d.

And also a lease from the Mayor and Commonality and Citizens of London Governors of St. Bartholomew's Hospital, to the said Sir Henry Marten, of a tenement called the Peacock and two messuages adjoining for thirty-one years at the yearly rent of £10.

And also a lease from the warden and scholars of St. Mary College, of Winchester, (in Oxford commonly called New College) in Oxford, to the said Sir Henry Marten, (dated 19th July, 14th Charles) of nine messuages in Petty Wales for the term of forty years, under the rent and covenants therein expressed.

It is witnessed that the said Henry Marten, in consideration of £1376 to him paid by the said Dame Mary Rogers, and of £624 to be paid as therein mentioned, did assign unto the said Dame Mary Rogers

"The said three several recited indentures of lease and the
"messuages or tenements in them demised for the remainder of
"the several terms therein granted"

28th September, 1652.

The said Dame Mary Rogers assigns unto Edmund Denton, his executors, administrators and assigns

"A moiety of her messuage called the church-house in
"Aldersgate Street and a moiety of nine messuages cottages or
"tenements situate in Petty Wales"

To hold unto the said Edmund Denton, his executors, administrators and assigns, for the remainder of the terms under which they were held.

NOTE.—Mr. Edmund Denton married Elizabeth Rogers, the youngest daughter of the said Dame Mary Rogers.

21st September, 1654.

The said Dame Mary Rogers assigns unto the said Edmund Denton

"The other moiety of the church-house and of the nine mes-
"suages cottages or tenements in Petty Wales"

To hold unto the said Edmund Denton, his executors, administrators and assigns, for the remainder of the several terms under which they were held.

17th October, 1657.

The said Edmund Denton, by his Will, devised all his leases to William Denton, Edward Trist, and Alexander Denton, John Smith, and George Underwood

Upon trust that the same should be sold by them, or the survivors or survivor of them, or the heirs of such survivor, for the best price that could be got for the same, and the money to be applied for payment of his debts.

30th April, 1658.

The executors of the said Edmund Denton assign this lease
To James Fletcher and several other parishioners of St. Botolph.

In trust for the parish

The former lease was surrendered, and on

7th September, 1661,

The warden and scholars of New College in Oxford demised these premises
To Cornelius Bee and William Pease, from Michaelmas, 1660, for forty years at £8 per annum.

And on

14th September, same year,

The said Cornelius Bee and William Pease assign the said lease
To James Fletcher and several others

In trust for the parish.

OBSERVATIONS.

These premises are described in the Trust Deed as 128 *and* 129 *Aldersgate Street, and were formerly known as the Church-house.*

They were acquired at various times; part appears to have come to the possession of the parish in 1384 *by a grant from John de Thornton to William Clophull and five other Trustees, but in* 1547, *by virtue of an Act of Parliament passed in the first year of the reign of Edward the 6th, intituled "An Act whereby certain chantries, colleges, free chapels, and the possessions of the same, be given to the King's Majesty." This, with the rest of the parish property, fell into the King's hands.*

On the 30th March, 1591, *Queen Elizabeth grants to William*

Tipper and Robert Dawe these premises who convey them to Trustees for the Parish; and they have, with the other property of the Parish, continued since to be conveyed to new Trustees.

On 12th February, 1613, King James granted a Commission to enquire of all lands and hereditaments belonging to the Crown not charged before the Auditor of the Exchequer, with a schedule of the said lands annexed thereto.

And by an Inquisition, the Jurors (amongst other things) found the yearly value of the lands and hereditaments belonging to this Parish to be £1 2s. 10d., to be paid yearly to the Crown as follows:—

	s.	d.
The Church House	3	4
Alain Johnson's House	3	0
The Five Shops	1	8
Two houses east of the Church	2	0
Three houses north of the Church	3	0
The Minister's house	1	4
Maidenhead Alley	1	4
Black Horse Alley	5	8
Necton's house	1	6
£1	2	10

Part were purchased by the Parishioners with the money derived from the sale of the property given by Mr. Tamworth, and other monies; and upon which premises his Gift, £33 6s. 8d. per annum, is charged. They came into the possession of the Parish on 1st November, 1658. See *Tamworth's Gift.*

And part are held under an Indenture of lease from the Wardens and Scholars of New College, Oxford, at the yearly rent of £8 8s. 0d.

The first lease is dated 19th July, 1638, and was assigned to the Trustees of the Parish on 30th April, 1658, and has been renewed from time to time. The present one will expire in 1881

The value at March, 1865, was £340 per annum, and are let under four leases as follows, viz.:—

Mr. Haven Kaye, under a lease for 21 years commencing 24th June, 1852, and expiring 24th June, 1873, at a yearly rental of - - - - - 130 0 0

Messrs. P. & J. Arnold, under a lease for 21 years commencing 29th September, 1851, and expiring 29th September, 1872, at a yearly rental of - - - 25 0 0

Mr. J. T. Norris (Petty Wales), under a lease for 21 years from 29th September, 1855, and expiring 29th September, 876, at a yearly rental of - - 80 0 0

Mr. J. T. Norris (New Street, Cloth Fair), for same term at a yearly rental of - - - - 105 0 0

Total - **£340 0 0**

After payment of the ground rent to New College, Oxford, of £8 8s. 0d., and Tamworth's Gift of £33 6s. 8d. per annum; the residue is applied to the repairs of the Church and the general purposes of the Parish.

These properties are now so amalgamated, and the descriptions so varied, that I cannot give the value of each at the date of acquisition. They were formerly as a whole styled "the Church House," and in 1659 were let to a Mr. Hills at £60 per annum.

Tenements in Aldersgate Street, formerly the inheritance of Alleyne Johnson.

16th June, 1498.

WILL OF ALLEYNE JOHNSON whereby (among other things) he bequeathed to Margaret his wife, for her life—This messuage, with the garden and appurtenances, in the parish of St. Botolph, and after her decease to the parson of the parish church of St. Botolph, and his successors, upon condition that the parson and churchwardens should keep an obit, after his death, for his soul, his father's, mother's, Jean's, his wife, and Margaret, after her death, and to spend at such obit. yearly 10s., to wit:—

To the parson, or his deputy - -	12d.	
To 4 priests each 4d. - • - -	16d.	
Parish clerk, for ringing the bell - -	8d.	7s. 8d.
For wax candle at the obit - - -	8d.	
For bread, ale, and cheese - - -	2s.	
To each of the wardens 12d. - -	2s.	
In alms to the poor - - - - -		2s. 4d.

And if the parson and wardens should make default, his house was to go to his right heirs for ever.

If his wife Margaret did not accept of his personal estate for her part, according to his bequest, and the custom of London, he bequeathed his said house, at his decease, to the said parson and his successors for ever, upon the condition aforesaid.—[Extracted from the register of the Bishop of London.]

2nd March, 1500. 15 Henry 7th.

BY INQUISITION, taken after the death of the said Alleyn Johnson, it was found That he was seized of the said messuage and garden, with the appurtenances, and that he made his Will as above; and after his death the said Margaret entered therein, and then held the same. That the premises were worth yearly, above reprizes, 33s. 4d. That he died on 26th June, 13 Henry 7th, and that William Fylard was his cousin, and next heir.

The said Margaret died in 1510, Upon whose death the said tenements were taken by the rector and wardens of the parish of St. Botolph, according to the Will.

1547. These premises fell in the King's hands by virtue of the statute of 1 Edward 6th of Chantries.

1st and 2nd Philip and Mary, 1553.

The Dean of Westminster, as rector of this parish, and the churchwardens, being charged in the accounts of the Receivers of the Court of Augmentation and Revenues of the Crown with five years and a-half arrears of rent of the said tenement (from 1st Edward 6th and ending Michaelmas, 1st Mary) the rector and wardens (in a cause between the King and Queen against said rector and wardens) pleaded to be discharged from the payment of such arrears, except from the payment of the 7s. 8d. yearly, which had been appointed for obits, &c., whereupon the Barons of the Exchequer decreed they should only pay 7s. 8d. yearly for ever to the Crown out of the rents of the said tenements.

12th February, 1613. 11th James.

By a Commission from King James, out of the Exchequer, upon the statute of 1st Edward 6th of Chantries, to enquire of lands, &c., not charged before the Auditor of the Exchequer. Upon the Inquisition thereon taken the jurors found that the premises formerly of Alleyn Johnson (among others) were part of the possessions of the King, by right of his Crown, and that the yearly value was 3s., to be paid yearly to the Crown.

14th January, 1614. 12th James.

King James, by letters patent, grants these premises (among others) to Edmund Duffield and John Babbington, in fee farm.

12th February, following.

The said Edmund Duffield and John Babbington grant these premises (among others) to William Willford and Nicholas Wilson, and their heirs, In trust for the parish.

Easter Term, 1619.

THE parishioners of St. Botolph exhibit their Bill in Chancery against the Dean and Chapter of Westminster, and their tenants, concerning the rents of these and other premises, which the Dean and Chapter had retained for some years, and on 11th November following, It was decreed that the rents to grow due during the lease thereof should be paid to the churchwardens and their successors, and that the arrears should be forthwith paid by the lessee and his assigns to the Plaintiffs.

1649. The lands of the Dean and Chapter of Westminster being to be sold by virtue of an Act for Sale of the Lands of Deans and Chapters, these houses were surveyed as belonging to the said Dean and Chapter. And thereupon the parishioners of St. Botolph Without Aldersgate put in their claim to these lands, which was opposed by one Helen Merchant, who pretended an interest in them by virtue of a lease from the Dean and Chapter, And on 21st February, 1649, it was ordered by the trustees for the sale of Deans' and Chapters' Land, That the business should be referred to Mr. Recorder Steele, and Mr. Martin, the counsel of the said trustees, And they were desired to state and report the matter, with their opinion thereon.

Whereupon Mr. Recorder and Mr. Martin certified:

1. That the tenement in question was the right of the said parish by the demise of Allan Johnson, to the rector of that parish and his successors, whereby he became seized to the use of the parish by the custom of London, and accordingly joined with the churchwardens in making several leases rendering rent to the use of the parish, which the churchwardens received. And the last lease made by the Dean and Chapter as rector, together with the churchwardens, was 33 Elizabeth, for sixty years, not yet elapsed, the title of Merchant being under Conyers, a lessee from the Dean and Chapter; and the parish, by reason of some difference with the parish, took a new lease, 9 James, from the Dean and Chapter alone, which gave rise first to this difference.

2. That supposing the Will of Allan Johnson to be a superstitious use, Duffield and Babbington became seized thereof by the patent, and their title was since come to the parish.

3. That by a Decree in Chancery, 1619, not yet reversed, an order was only made to interrupt the payment of the rents.

They were therefore of opinion that the title of the said parish was not impeached by anything alleged on behalf of the said Merchant.

After the making of this Certificate, the parishioners made their entry in the said houses, and sealed a lease of ejectment, and obtained judgment against the ejectors in the Lord Mayor's Court.

15th May, 1656.

THE COMMISSIONERS for removing obstructions in the sale of Deans' and Chapters' Lands ordered and adjudged:

"That the right title and interest of the churchwardens and parishioners claimed by them to the said three tenements be allowed of unto them, the said churchwardens, and their successors, churchwardens and parishioners of the said parish; and that they do hold, and ought so to hold, and enjoy the same, and the rents and profits thereof, for the charitable uses aforesaid. And that no sale be or ought to be made of the said messuages and their appurtenances, or any of them, for the use of the Commonwealth. And that the Surveyor General for Sale of Deans' and Chapters' Lands do therefore enter and record, upon the survey of the premises, the claim and interest of the said churchwardens and parishioners to the premises allowed of hereby accordingly."

OBSERVATIONS.

These premises were formerly known as "Alleyne Johnson's Houses," and appear to have first come into possession of the parish upon the death of Margaret Johnson in 1510. As there are no Churchwardens' accounts until 1637, I cannot state the value at the date of acquisition, except that by the Inquisition of King James before set forth; it appears to have been £1 13s. 4d. per annum.

It is now let to Mr. George Ellwood, who holds the same under two leases, one of which is for 61 years from 24th June 1860, and expires 24th June, 1921, at a yearly rent of £40; the other for 71 years commencing from 24th June 1860, and expiring 24th June, 1931, at a yearly rent of £176

The value at March 1865 was **£216** per annum, which is applied for the repairs of the Church, and general purposes of the parish.

TRINITY HALL.

This property appears to have come into the hands of the parish in the year 1561, as the following Deeds set forth.

4th July, 1561. *3rd of Elizabeth.*

By Deed Poll thus dated Richard Emerson, being religiously moved, and for a certain sum of money to him paid, did give grant and confirm unto John Melsham and seventeen other Citizens of the City of London and parishioners of the parish of St. Botolph without Aldersgate London

"All that his messuage house and tenement called the Trinity Hall otherwise the common Hall of the Fraternity or Guild of the Holy Trinity founded in the Church of St. Botolph without Aldersgate London aforesaid dissolved and the kitchen and buttery to the same belonging and then occupied with the same And also free ingress and regress in and to the said messuage and tenement by the way then leading from Aldersgate Street aforesaid to the stairs of the Hall of the said messuage by the gate called the gate leading to the Trinity Hall, with all the lights to the said messuage kitchen and buttery then being and as they were occupied by the parishioners of the said parish.

(Except certain chambers built over the kitchen aforesaid and the lower part of the said Hall then late in the tenure or occupation of Thomas Farnham Gent. with the buildings to the said chambers belonging and appertaining which he had of the grant of William Harvie, who had them of the grant of King Edward the VI.

To hold to said Melsham and others (except as aforesaid) their heirs and assigns for ever

To be held of the Queen her heirs and successors by fealty in free soccage and not in capite

With general warranty

Executed by Richard Emerson
Livery of Seisin indorsed

Same date.

BY INDENTURE between the said Richard Emerson of the one part, and John Melsham and John Long of the other part, The said Richard Emerson, in consideration of £45, did bargain and sell, give and grant, to said Melsham and Long

> The before mentioned premises (except as before excepted) and all right. &c., And all deeds which he covenanted to deliver before Michaelmas then next,

To hold to the said John Melsham and John Long, their heirs and assigns for ever

Covenant from Richard Emerson, that he was lawfully seized and had power to bargain and sell

And for further assurance

And against all incumbrances

And also that all feoffees should stand seized thereof to the same uses

And for all other assurances

And for quiet enjoyment by them or their assignees

Same date.

BOND FOR PERFORMANCE OF COVENANT.

2nd June, 1582. 24th *Elizabeth.*

By deed poll thus dated, William Fyssher, Richard Everingham, John Fustenaunce, Dunstan Bilby, John Fyssher, and Henry Binforth, citizens of the City of London, and parishioners of the parish church of St. Botolph Without Aldersgate, after reciting a grant of Richard Emerson to Melsham and Long, of 4th July, 1561, of Trinity Hall, (except the lower part thereof) continues as follows, viz. :—

> " The which grant and feoffment was so had and made as is
> " aforesaid for and to the intent that the same messuage tenement
> " house and other the premises might be had and used as a common
> " hall and place for the assemblies of the churchwardens and other
> " officers and parishioners of and within the same parish for the
> " more commodious meetings and assemblies when and as often as
> " they for their common causes should have occasion so to meet or
> " assemble,"

And reciting that the said John Melsham and John Long had ordered that when all the said feoffees save seven or six should die, the survivors should renew the feoffment of the said messuage, house, and tenement, to other eleven or twelve persons of the same parish, to be named always by the churchwardens for the time being, or by twelve of the most discreet and honest persons of the same parish which had been churchwardens there, to the intent that the freehold and inheritance of the same might for ever remain in a competent number of feoffees, inhabitants of the same parish, and to be used so as aforesaid, As by a writing thereof in a table or frame hung up in the church for a perpetual memory of the premises. Dated 8th July, 3rd Elizabeth, 1561.

The said William Fisher, and others, did grant, bargain, sell, enfeoff, deliver, and confirm to John Sotherton and twenty-three other parishioners of the said parish

"The said premises (except as before excepted) To hold to them their heirs and assigns for ever

"To be holden of the Chief Lords of the fee, with General warrantry

"Livery of Seisen endorsed."

The following Deed conveys to the trustees of the parish that part of the Trinity Hall which is excepted in the former deeds.

20th November, 1655.

By INDENTURE between the Mayor and Commonality and Citizens of of the City of London, Governors of the possessions, revenues and goods of the hospitals of Edward the 6th, of Christ's Bridewell, and St. Thomas the Apostle, of the one part, and John Micklethwayte and twenty-two other parishioners of the other part.

It is witnessed that for ending all differences between the parties, touching the right and title of the cellar and room aftermentioned, And in consideration of £25, the said Mayor and Commonality did bargain and sell to the said John Micklethwayte, and others

One room now used for a kitchen, containing in length from north to south fifteen feet of assize (little more or less), and in breadth from east to west 10 feet of assize (little more or less.)

One parlour on the east side of the said kitchen, on the same floor, containing in length from north to south sixteen feet of assize and four inches (little more or less), and in breadth from east to west fifteen feet of assize (little more or less), lying and being under Trinity Hall, or the Quest House in Trinity Court, in Aldersgate Street, London, belonging to the said parish.

One cellar under the said parlour, containing in length from north to south fourteen feet of assize (little more or less), and from east to west twelve feet of assize (little more or less.)

And one yard paved with freestone, containing from north to south eleven feet of assize and four inches, and from east to west eight feet of assize (little more or less.) Together with all ways and passages out of the said court into and from the said bargained premises, and every part thereof, with all other ways, passages, staircases, and easements into and from the said Quest House, or any room or rooms belonging to the same, with all their and every of their appurtenances. All which said premises, are situate, lying and being in Aldersgate Street and Trinity Court aforesaid, in the parish aforesaid, and are in the several tenures and occupations of John Wright and Thomas Carter, or one of them, their or one of their assignee or assigns.

Together with all deeds, writings, evidences, escripts, counterparts of leases, rentals, surveys, and muniments touching or concerning only the said bargained premises, or only any part or parcel thereof, and true copies of all such other writings as concern the same, with any other which are in the custody of the said Mayor and Commonality and Citizens Governors aforesaid

Except and always reserved out of this present grant, bargain, sale, and re-lease, unto and for the said Mayor and Commonality and Citizens of London aforesaid, their successors and assigns for ever, 'All that watercourse and pipe of lead coming from the same, and now belonging or appertaining with the messuage or tenement of the said Mayor, &c., adjoining on the east side of the yard, hereby granted and now in the tenure or occupation of Sarah Austin, widow, or her assigns, and which falleth into the said paved yard, and which now are used and enjoyed with the said messuage or tenement by the tenants or occupiers thereof, with free liberty of ingress, regress, and egress to and for the said Mayor and Commonality and Citizens of London aforesaid, their tenants, workmen and assigns from time to time, and at all seasonable and convenient times for ever hereafter to come into the said paved yard to amend the watercourse and pipe coming from the said messuage through the said paved yard, they the said Mayor, &c., their successors and assigns from time to time, and at all times from henceforth for ever, well and sufficiently keeping and repairing the said watercourse and pipe so as it may be no nuisance or damage to the said bargained premises.

To hold to them, their heirs and assigns, for ever.

Covenant for peaceable enjoyment.

Power to William Parry to enter the premises and deliver possession thereof to said feoffees. Power for the Mayor, &c., to enjoy the lights in the paved alley.

Seisen endorsed.

This, with other properties belonging to the parish, have been from time to time conveyed by similar deeds of feoffment (trust deeds) to new feoffees (trustees) by the survivors.

The last trust deed dated 17th November, 1865, is fully set forth at p. 128.

OBSERVATIONS.

The property conveyed by the first Deed appears to have been originally let on lease to the Farriers' Company in 1612 at £4 per annum, and the premises comprised in the 2nd Deed to have been first let also at £4 per annum.

These properties are still in the possession of the parish, and are now known as 165, 166, and 167, Aldersgate Street.

No. 165 is now held on two leases by the City of London Literary and Scientific Institution, but in the occupation of the Young Men's Christian Association for the term of 61 years from 29th September 1837, at the rents of £10 and £20. It appears in the Churchwardens' accounts as "Executors of G. Stacey."

Nos. 166 and 167 are let on lease to Thomas Jones, deceased, for the term of 61 years from Michaelmas 1837, at a yearly rent of £80, which premises are now occupied by Messrs. Gough & Nettleship.

The values at the respective dates of acquisition was £4 and £4 per annum, and at March 1865 the value of the whole was **£110** per annum, which is appropriated for the repair and keeping up of the church, and the general purposes of the parish.

THE MINISTER'S HOUSE.

The upper part of this house consisted of rooms and lodgings for two priests, and the lower part thereof was a Charnel House.

This house also fell to the Crown by the Statute of Chantries, and was conveyed, with the Church-house and other premises, to the parish by William Tipper and Robert Dawe in 1594.

This tenement is described in the Commission granted by King James in the year 1613 for concealed lands, to be situate, lying, and being in the Churchyard, and then or then late in the tenure of Simon Kingsland or his assigns, and was granted by said King James to Edmund Duffield and John Babbington in 1614, and by them in the same year conveyed to William Wilford and Nicholas Wilson in trust for the parish, paying yearly therefore to the Crown 16d.

It is comprised in all the feoffments made since that time with the Church-house, &c.

This house was new built, at the charge of the parish, in the year 1628, and let to the then minister of this parish for his habitation, and for some time after was occupied by the Minister for the time being by leases for seven years.

OBSERVATIONS.

These premises are situate in Little Britain, and, as far as I can trace, appear to be now in the occupation of Mr. Fowler, under a lease of 21 years commencing 25th March, 1860, and expiring 25th March, 1881, at a yearly rental of £42, and are fully set forth fifthly and sixthly in the Trust Deed.

It appears by the above to have (after the Act of Edward the 6th before mentioned) first belonged to the parish in the year 1594.

I cannot state the value at acquisition, but at March 1865 it was **£42** *per annum, which is applied to the repairs of the Church and general purposes of the parish.*

Maidenhead Alley, otherwise Lamb Alley.

26th September, 1392. *16th Richard 2nd.*

KING RICHARD 2nd, in consideration of 100s. paid by John de Thornton, grants license to said John de Thornton to give in mortmain a messuage, with the appurtenances, in the parish of St. Botolph Without Aldersgate, To hold to the parson of the church of St. Botolph, and his successors for ever, for maintaining certain charges in the church aforesaid, according to the ordinance of the said parson.

27th September, 1392.

The said John de Thornton grants to the parson of the church of St. Botolph Without Aldersgate, The said house in Aldersgate Street, To hold to him and his successors, for certain charges to be maintained, for ever, according to his ordinance, and according to the form of the charter granted thereof by King Richard 2nd.

4th September, 1395. *19th Richard 2nd.*

Ralph de Kestenen, parson of the church of St. Botolph, reciting the King's license to John de Thornton, and that he had full seisin of the said house, Ordains for him and his successors, that the rents thereof be paid by the parson to the wardens of the said church for the time being, in aid and support of the fabrick and ornaments and other necessaries of St. Botolph aforesaid for ever.

1547. These premises likewise fell in the King's hands by virtue of the Statute of Chantries.

This house or ground was conveyed in the same manner as the church-house, Black Horse Alley, rector's house, and the minister's house, viz. :—

30th March, 1591,

Grant from Queen Elizabeth to William Tipper and Robert Dawe.

23rd May, 1594,

Grant from Tipper and Dawe to John Sotherton, and others.

12th February, 1613,

The Commission and Inquisition by which it is found that the premises were part of the possessions of the King, in right of his Crown.

14th January, 1614,

Grant from King James to Edmund Duffield and John Babbington

20th February, 1614,

Grant from Duffield and Babbington to William Willford and Nicholas Wilson, In trust for the parish.

A piece of Ground and Tenement in Lamb Alley, adjoining the other tenement in the said Alley, purchased by the parish for the use of a workhouse.

1st and 2nd October, 1765.

By INDENTURES of lease and re-lease, between John Taylor of Winchester Street, London, bricklayer, of the one part, and Thomas Bywater, of the parish of St. Botolph Without Aldersgate, London, Thomas Serjeant and George Lewis Carr of the same parish

It is witnessed, that in consideration of £210, to the said John Taylor paid by the said Bywater, Serjeant, and Carr, for the absolute purchase of the fee simple, &c. The said John Taylor did grant, bargain, sell, alien, re-lease and confirm, unto the said Bywater, Serjeant, and Carr, their heirs and assigns

All that new built brick messuage or tenement of him the said John Taylor situate standing and being on the south side of Maidenhead Court in the said parish of St. Botolph Without Aldersgate London and the ground and soil whereon the same doth stand which said messuage or tenement was lately rebuilt by the said John Taylor upon the ground on which an old messuage or tenement lately stood and which was lately in the tenure or occupation of or made use of by the officers of the said parish of St. Botolph for the reception of some of the poor of the said parish being contiguous and near adjoining to the workhouse belonging to the said parish And which new brick messuage or tenement and premises now are or late were in the tenure or occupation of John Couchman together with all yards backsides sheds outhouses cellars sollars chambers lights easements ways passages waters and watercourses profits commodities hereditaments and appurtenances whatsoever to the said messuage or tenement ground hereditaments and premises belonging or in anywise appertaining or therewith used occupied or enjoyed or accepted reputed or taken as part parcel or member thereof

And the reversion, &c.

And all the estate, &c.

And all deeds, &c., and copies "

To hold to them their heirs and assigns for ever
   Covenant that he is lawfully seized and hath good right to convey
   Power of entry and perception of rents
   Free from incumbrances
   And for further assurances
   And a covenant for production of deeds and writings
        Executed by John Taylor and receipt for £210 indorsed

OBSERVATIONS.

It would appear from the above that these premises came into the possession of the parish at various times, the first-mentioned part in the year 1392, and, with other property, fell into the King's hands by virtue of the Statute of Chantries, but was, as above, again granted to the parish.

I have no means of ascertaining the value at the date of acquisition, but in 1637, according to the first Churchwardens' accounts, it was let at a yearly rent of £1 15s.

The last-mentioned part was purchased in the year 1765, of Mr. John Taylor, for the sum of £210 as above stated.

We have in our possession at the present time Nos. 4, 5, 6, & 7, Maidenhead Court, and the premises are now let as follows:

No. 4. On lease to Mr. John Reynolds for a term of 21 years commencing 24th June, 1861, and terminating 24th June, 1882, at a yearly rent of - - - 26 0 0

No. 5. On a lease to Mr. Albert Glover for 21 years, commencing 24th June, 1867, expiring 24th June, 1888, at a yearly rental of - - - - - - 40 0 0

No. 6. On lease to Mr. William Welch for 21 years, commencing 25th December, 1862, terminating 25th December 1883, at a yearly rent of - - - 25 0 0

No. 7. On lease to Mr. John Aitcheson for 21 years, commencing 24th June, 1859, and expiring 24th June, 1880, at a yearly rental of - - - - - 48 0 0

Making the total yearly value at March 1865 - **139 0 0**

Which is likewise applied for the Church and general purposes of the parish.

Black Horse, otherwise Little Horse Alley, in Aldersgate Street.

17th June, 1478. 17th Edward 4th.

BY FEOFFMENT, Nicholas Dudley and John Jacob grant unto William Hall, and Joan his wife

"The north side of the said alley with the house of office at the west end of the said alley (reserving to John Aylwyn the use of the house of office and of the well) And also 1d. annual rent payable by Aylwyn"

To hold to the said William Hall and Joan his wife for their lives and the life of the survivor of them remainder

To Margery Domegood daughter of said William Hall and the heirs of her body remainder

To the rector of St Botolph and the wardens of said parish

In trust to be sold

And with the money arising by such sale to pay

60s. for 6 torches in said church

60s. for 6 torches in St. Olave's Southwark

60s. to Catherine sister of said William Hall

100s. for coals for 5 years to the poor in Aldersgate

100s. for the same purpose in St. Olave's parish

And the residue of the money to be paid to the said rector and wardens for keeping an obit for the said William and his relations and friends Such expence to be 20s. viz.:—

To the rector priests and clerks - - 4s.
Bread cheese and ale - - - - - 2s. 8d.
To the poor of said parish - - - - 13s. 4d.

14th April, 1488. *4th Henry 7th.*

By feoffment Nicholas Dudley (who survived John Jacob) grants unto Nicholas Lathell and nineteen others

"All the lands and premises in Aldersgate parish which he with "John Jacob had of the grant of William Hall"

To hold to them their heirs and assigns for ever With power of attorney to enter and deliver possession

1547. 1*st Edward* 6*th.*

These premises fell in the King's hands by virtue of the statute of 1st Edward 6th of Chantries

30*th March,* 1591. 34*th Elizabeth.*

The Queen grants these premises (among others) to William Tipper and Robert Dawe their heirs and assigns

And by other Letters Patent also grants all fee farms, annuities, pensions, rents, &c.

23rd *May,* 1594,

The said William Tipper and Robert Dawe grant these premises (with others) to John Sotherton and others And by another deed released all fee farm rents due out of the said premises

12*th February,* 1613. 11*th James,*

A Commission was awarded out of the Exchequer upon the Statute of 1st Edward 6th of Chantries, to enquire of the lands in the schedule annexed, whereof these premises were part, And it was found by Inquisition that they were part of the possessions of the King in right of his Crown

14*th January,* 1614. 12*th James.*

King James, by Letters Patent, grants these premises (among others) to Edmund Duffield and John Babbington and their heirs in fee farm.

20th February, 1611,

The said Edmund Duffield and John Babbington grant these premises (among others) to William Willford and Nicholas Wilson, their heirs and assigns for ever

In trust for the parish.

Same date.

And by another deed re-leased to them All the rents and arrears of rent due out of the same.

From that time these premises were conveyed by feoffments, with the church house and several other premises of the parish.

The ground contained in breadth forty feet, and in length ninety-eight feet. And these were eighteen tenements. And the total of the yearly rents amounted per annum to £45 17s. 0d

A tenement next to Black Horse Alley, formerly demised upon a building lease to William Necton.

N.B.—It appears by the following deeds, that in 19th Henry 7th, one Edmund Burton recovered in the Hustings Court of London, against John Croke the younger (amongst others), a messuage and garden and 8s. rent in the parish of St. Botolph Without Aldersgate.

There are no records of this recovery, nor any transcript of such record.

22nd May, 1509. *1st Henry 8th.*

Thomas Croke re-leases to Edmund Burton

"All his right and title to three messuages one garden and 8s. rent, two whereof are situate in the parish of St. Bridget and the other with the garden in the parish of St. Botolph Without Aldersgate which said Burton had recovered against John Croke his brother in the 19th Henry 7th"

With general warranty.

26th May, same year.

The said Edmund Burton grants

"The same premises which he had recovered against John
"Croke"

To William Britayn, William Aylmer, and Thomas Langridge, their heirs and assigns for ever.

With Livery of Seisin.

29th August, same year.

The said Edmund Burton re-leases to them

"All his right, &c. thereto"

Same date.

Thomas Croke also re-leases to them
"All his right, &c. with general warranty"

11th November, 1516. 8th Henry 8th.

The said William Britayn, William Aylmer, and Thomas Langridge, by feoffment, grant to Richard Sheldon and fourteen other parishioners of St. Botolph, for £24 sterling

"A messuage and garden and 8s. rent in Aldersgate Street which
"they had of Edmund Burton"

To hold to them their heirs and assigns for ever.

1547. These premises likewise fell in the King's hands by virtue of the Statute of 1st Edward 6th of Chantries.

30th March, 1591. 34th Elizabeth.

Queen Elizabeth, by Letters Patent, grants this tenement (among others) to William Tipper and Robert Dawe, their heirs and assigns.

And also granted all fee farms, annuities, &c. which ought to have been paid to her out of the same.

23rd May, 1594,

The said Tipper and Dawe convey the said premises to John Sotherton and others, their heirs and assigns for ever. And by another deed release the same to them and to the successors of the rector and churchwardens of the said parish.

11th James, 1613,

A Commission is awarded out of the Exchequer upon the Statute of Chantries, to inquire of the lands in a schedule thereto annexed, whereof these premises are part. And it is found by Inquisition that these premises were part of the possessions of the King in right of his Crown.

14th January, 1614.

King James, by Letters Patent, grants these premises (among others) to Edmund Duffield and John Babbington in fee farm.

20th February, 1614.

The said Duffield and Babbington grant the same to William Willford and Nicholas Wilson in fee, In trust for the parish.

And by another deed of the same date, re-leased to them All the rents and arrears due out of the same.

6th June, 1586.

The rector and churchwardens demised this ground to William Necton for ninety-nine years, at the yearly rent of £3 5s. 8d.

The dimensions are therein mentioned to be On the south part thereof in length from the street side by the north side of the tenement and garden of the said William Necton unto the east end of the said messuage of Robert Burgayne eighty-four feet one inch of assize, and in breadth from the north corner of the garden of the said William Necton by the east end of the said messuage of the said Robert Burgayne unto the south corner of the said tenement parcel of Black Horse Alley twenty feet of assize. And in length from the said east end of the messuage of Mr. Burgayne, by the south side of the said tenements of the said parish in Black Horse Alley into Aldersgate Street eighty-three feet one inch of assize And from the south corner of the said tenements of the parish in Black Horse Alley by the said street into the north corner of the tenement of said Necton nineteen feet two inches of assize.

N B.—This house and Mr. Necton's own house were new built in the year 1589, and were one entire house, but Mr. Necton's part was marked with the letters W. N., and the parish's part with S. B.

OBSERVATIONS.

The above premises are 8thly and 9thly described in the Trust Deed, and appear to have first virtually come into the possession of the parish by a Grant of Queen Elizabeth, dated 30th March, 1591.

They are described in the Trust Deed as Nos. 140, 141, *and two* other messuages and dwelling-houses in the rear thereof, and 142, Aldersgate Street.

I cannot give their value at the date of acquisition; but in 1637, according to the first Churchwardens' Accounts, they were let at a yearly rent of £13 6s. 8d.

They are now let on lease as follows:—

No. 140, to William Wray Cork, for 21 years commencing 25th March, 1852, and expiring 25th March, 1873, at a yearly rent of - - - - -   55 0 0

No. 141, to the executors of J. Hare, for 21 years commencing 25th December, 1851, and expiring 25th December, 1873, at a yearly rent of - - - 120 0 0

No. 142, to Richard Rayner, for 21 years commencing 29th September, 1864, and expiring 29th September, 1885, at a yearly rent of - - - -   85 0 0

Making (at March, 1865) a total yearly value of - £260 0 0

Which is applied for the repairs of the church and general purposes of the Parish.

A Tenement in Doelittle Lane in the Parish of St. Mary Magdalen, Old Fish Street, London.

23rd March, 1603. 1*st James.*

EDWARD VAUGHAN (by Deed enrolled in London) Grants to Nowell Sotherton Esquire his heirs and assigns for ever.

" The tenement in the parish of St Mary Magdalen in Old Fish
" Street. And the tenement in Bread Street."

15th April, 1604.

The said Nowell Sotherton (by bargain and sale grants to John Sotherton Esquire and thirty-one other parishioners of this parish

" The said two tenements"

To hold to them their heirs and assigns for ever.

29th March, 1633.

Feoffment from Christopher Sotherton Esquire to John New, Roger Taylor, and John Edwards, (the surviving Feoffees in the last deed.)

" Reciting the last Feoffment of April 15th, 1604.

And that John Sotherton Esquire Nowell Sotherton and William Necton by deed of 7th March 2nd Charles did enfeoff Thomas Pagitt and several other parishioners of the said parish and their heirs and assigns for ever of Trinity Hall with the appurtenances And as all and every the same feoffees in said deed named were dead except the said Christopher Sotherton John New Roger Taylor and John Edwards"

They therefore enfeoffed Sir Henry Martyn knight and twenty-seven others of the said parish, trustees to the poor of the said parish, and to their heirs and assigns for ever

" The said tenement in Old Fish Street The tenement in Bread
" Street and the messuage tenement and house called Trinity Hall"

16th *September*, 1659.

By an order of vestry reciting that they had agreed to sell the tenement in Bread Street to Samuel Houghton for £80. They desired and entreated Henry Marten and James Acton for the consideration of £80 to convey unto the said Samuel Houghton in fee all their interest in the same and agreed to save them harmless for so doing.

13th *April*, 1661.

Henry Marten Esquire (by deed poll) reciting that he with James Acton by virtue of a feoffment to them and others dated 29th March 1633 of whom the said Henry Marten and James Acton were the survivors and stood seized to them and their heirs (but in trust and for the only benefit of the parishioners of the said parish) of the said messuage in the parish of St. Mary Magdalene in Old Fish Street aforesaid and of Trinity Hall At the request of the parishioners of said parish did demise release and for ever quit claim unto the said James Acton his heirs and assigns for ever

> "All his right title &c. to the said premises to the use of the "said James Acton his heirs and assigns for ever"

1st *August*, 1672.   13th *Charles* 2nd.

James Acton (the surviving trustee) by deed inrolled in the Common Pleas grants

> The said tenements

To Miles Flesher, Nathaniel Nowell, and several others, their heirs and assigns for ever

> In trust for the poor of the said parish.

OBSERVATIONS

The above premises are tenthly and eleventhly fully set forth in the Trust Deed, and are let as follows :

One tenement to Charles Godwin on a lease for 21 *years from September,* 1848, *to September,* 1869, *at a yearly rent of* £19

One tenement to the executors of Mr. William Philp on a lease for 21 years from September, 1848, to September, 1869, at a yearly rent of £21

One tenement to the executors of Mr. Powell on a yearly tenancy of £12 per annum.

They were acquired by purchase in 1604.

I cannot give the value at the date of acquisition; but at March, 1865, they were of the yearly value of £52, which is applied for the repairs of the Church and general purposes of the Parish.

They are subject to a charge of £5. See Mrs. Hibben's Gift, p. 113.

Mr. MATTHEW KEMPSTER'S GIFT

MATTHEW KEMPSTER by his Will, dated 31st August 1624 devised to the Company of Tallow-chandlers, and their successors, four messuages, situate near Dowgate, in the Parish of St. John in Walbrook, in the City of London, upon trust therewith, among other charges, to pay the following yearly rents:

To the poor people of St. Botolph, Aldersgate, £1.

To the poor of the Company, £1.

The Company are in possession, under this gift, of three houses on the east side of Dowgate-hill, let to James Richardson, at the yearly rent of £100, and pay to the Churchwardens of St. Botolph Aldersgate, the sum of £1 yearly.

OBSERVATIONS

The sum of £1 annually receivable from the Tallow-chandlers' Company, is distributed in bread to the poor.

Mr. RICHARD OSMOTHERLAW'S GIFT.

———◆———

RICHARD OSMOTHERLAW, by Will, dated the 7th May, 1612, gave to the master and wardens of the Merchant Taylors, after the death of his wife, all the residue of his rents and profits whatsoever issuing out of his freehold lands and tenements in the parish of St. Botolph, Aldersgate, to hold to them, their successors and assigns, for ever, subject nevertheless to the following annuities, amongst others, at the feast of St. Philip and Jacob, viz. :

To five poor people inhabiting within the parish of St. Botolph, Aldersgate, 20d. a week, for ever, equally amongst them, such poor people to be nominated by the vestry of the said parish, and the money to be distributed by the churchwardens of the same parish.

To a godly preacher, for a sermon to be made in remembrance of the testator on the first Sunday in Lent, yearly, for ever, in the said parish church, 6s. 8d.

To the churchwardens aforesaid for the time being for ever, 4s. equally between them, for their pains in distributing the money to the five poor people.

To the clerk and sexton for the time being of the said parish 16d. a-piece yearly, for ever.

The property derived under the above Will consists of five houses, two in Aldersgate-street and three in Little Britain.

The sums given as above to the poor, the preacher, the church-wardens, clerk, and sexton of St. Botolph, would amount to £5 per annum; and the company have paid to the churchwardens of St. Botolph Aldersgate, the sum of £4 per annum only, to answer those bequests as far as the same would extend, according to their reduced proportions, £1 being deducted from the said £5 rent-charge for the land-tax.

OBSERVATIONS

The sum of £4 has been received yearly from the Merchant Taylors' Company, who in the terms of an order of the Charity Commissioners, dated the 18th of November 1873, transferred to the official trustees of Charitable funds the sum of £167 consols, the dividend on which (£5 per annum) receivable from the official trustees, is, less the payment above directed, distributed in bread to the poor.

1874.

PARISH PROPERTY.

Names of Tenants.	Premises.	Years.	Commencing.	Expiring.	Rent.	Names of Occupiers
Mr. William Webb	81, Little Britain	Yearly	24th June 1870		£62	Miss M. S. Gardiner, Sextoness
	5 & 6, Knightrider Court Doctors Commons					Mr. Wm. Webb
Messrs. P. & J. Arnold	Petty Wales (135, Aldersgate Street)	"	September 1872		£65	Messrs. P. & J. Arnold
Mr. Thomas Blake's Exors.	129, Aldersgate Street	3¾	24th June 1873	September 1876	£130	Mr. J. O. St. A. Angove and others
Mr. J. T. Norris's Assigns	Petty Wales (16, New Street)	21	September 1855	September 1876	£80	Mr. W. H. Collingridge's under-tenants
Ditto ditto	17, New St., Cloth Fair	21	September 1855	September 1876	£105	Mr. T. Brooks
Mr. John Aitcheson	7, Maidenhead Court	21	24th June 1869	24th June 1880	£48	Mr. William Welch
Mr. William Cave Fowler	77 & 77½, Little Britain	21	25th March 1860	25th March 1881	£42	No. 77, Mr. W. M. Rowell No. 77½, Mr. Samuel Parsey
Mr. John Reynolds' Exors	4, Maidenhead Court	21	24th June 1861	24th June 1882	£26	Mr. G. H. Smith's under-tenants
Mr. William Welch	6, Maidenhead Court	21	December 1862	December 1883	£25	Mr. Samuel Welch
Mr. Richd. Rayner's Exors.	142, Aldersgate Street	21	September 1864	September 1885	£85	Mr. H. A. Rayner
Mr. Joseph Francis	141, Aldersgate Street and 3 & 4, Bowman's Buildings	12¾	December 1872	September 1886	£250	Mr. Joseph Francis
Mr. Arthur John Saxon	140, Aldersgate Street	12½	25th March 1873	September 1885	£110	Mr. A. J. Saxon
Mr. Albert Glover	5, Maidenhead Court	21	24th June 1867	24th June 1888	£40	Mr. Albert Glover
Mr. G. Stacy's Executors.	165, Aldersgate Street	61	September 1837	September 1898	£30	The Young Men's Christian Association
Mr. T. Jones's Executors	166 & 167, Aldersgate Street	61	September 1837	September 1898	£80	Mr. W. E. Winkley and Mr. G. Nettleship
Mr. George Ellwood's Exors.	164, Aldersgate Street	61	24th June 1860	24th June 1921	£40	Mr. George Ellwood
Mr. George Ellwood's Exors.	164, Aldersgate Street	71	24th June 1860	24th June 1931	£176	Mr. George Ellwood

www.ingramcontent.com/pod-product-compliance
Lightning Source LLC
Chambersburg PA
CBHW032151160426
43197CB00008B/866